Langenscheidt

100 Briefe Englisch

Musterbriefe für die Geschäftskorrespondenz

von Birgit Abegg

und Michael Benford

Langenscheidt

Berlin · München · Wien · Zürich · New York

Die in den Musterbriefen verzeichneten Namen, Anschriften, Telefon- und Faxnummern sind mit einigen Ausnahmen fingiert. Die darin enthaltenen Warenpreise sind, da sie dauernden Schwankungen unterliegen, nicht als maßgebend anzusehen.

© 2000 by Langenscheidt KG, Berlin und München
Druck: Druckhaus Langenscheidt, Berlin-Schöneberg
Printed in Germany · ISBN 3-468-**41122**-7 · www.langenscheidt.de

Vorwort

Die vorliegenden Briefe wurden völlig neu gestaltet und in Inhalt, Stil und Form der heutigen Geschäftspraxis angepasst. Neben einer selbstverständlich auf den neuesten Stand gebrachten Einweisung in die Form des englischen Geschäftsbriefs werden auch die britischen und amerikanischen Postzustellsysteme, das Telefax und die E-Mail behandelt. Die einleitenden Kapitel enthalten auch wichtige Vermerke auf Briefen, Unterschiede zwischen britischem und amerikanischem Englisch sowie Kommentare zu Großschreibung, Silbentrennung und Zeichensetzung.

Den Musterbriefen selbst folgen am Ende einige nützliche Anhänge, sowie ein Verzeichnis wichtiger Handelsabkürzungen und eine Sammlung von Briefmustern und Briefumschlägen im Original-Layout. Ein ausführliches alphabetisches Sachregister am Ende erleichtert den schnellen Zugriff auf den gewünschten Brief oder Begriff.

Die Autoren dieser Neubearbeitung sind Birgit Abegg, staatlich anerkannte Übersetzerin und Gerichtsdolmetscherin, die seit langem in Firmen der deutschen Industrie auch als Dozentin für Wirtschaftssprachen tätig ist, und Michael Benford M. A., der seit vielen Jahren Wirtschaftsenglisch an einer Handelsschule unterrichtet. Beide Autoren sind im Prüfungsausschuss für den Bereich Englisch der Industrie- und Handelskammer zu Düsseldorf tätig.

Autoren und Redaktion möchten sich bei den namentlich genannten Firmen für die erhaltene Unterstützung sowie die Bereitstellung der Originalvorlagen bedanken.

LANGENSCHEIDT

Inhaltsverzeichnis

Die Form des englischen Geschäftsbriefes

Das Lay-out und die Bestandteile des englischen Geschäftsbriefes unterliegen gewissen Normen und Regeln, die teilweise von denen der deutschen DIN-Normen abweichen.

Die in diesem Zusammenhang relevante britische Publikation ist der "Guide for Typewriting", erarbeitet von der British Standards Institution*. Diese Broschüre vermittelt einen kurzen Einblick in alle Einzelheiten des Lay-outs und der Form eines Geschäftsbriefes in englischer Sprache. Sie beinhaltet u. a. auch Abkürzungen, Block- oder eingerückte Schreibform, Rechensymbole, die Schreibweise von Zahlen und Brüchen, Zeilenabstände usw.

Im Zeichen der EU werden in naher Zukunft Anpassungen der internationalen Normen und Regeln erfolgen, die zum Teil heute noch voneinander abweichen. Dies findet seinen ersten Ausdruck in bereits stattfindenden Sitzungen z.B. einzelner Handelskammern und Verbände, die damit beschäftigt sind, gemeinsame Richtlinien für Prüfungen und Ausbildungsabschlüsse zu verabschieden. Zum heutigen Zeitpunkt kann daher eine endgültige Form, die EU-verbindlich ist, noch nicht gegeben werden.

Die Form englischer Privatbriefe, vor allen Dingen handschriftlich geschriebener, unterliegt in einigen Punkten anderen Gepflogenheiten, Regeln und Normen. Der Langenscheidt-Titel *Dear Jenny… Dear Sir… – Englische Privatbriefe mit deutscher Übersetzung* bietet ausführliche Informationen zu diesem Thema.

Die zurzeit und im Zuge des Computerzeitalters bevorzugte Form des englischen Geschäftsbriefes besteht aus folgenden Teilen:

1. Briefkopf (letterhead)
2. Bezugszeile (reference line)
3. Datum (date)
4. Anschrift des Empfängers (inside address)
5. Anrede (salutation)
6. Betreff (subject line)
7. Brieftext (body of the letter)
8. Schlussformel (complimentary close)
9. Name und Unterschrift (name and signature)
10. Anlagen (enclosures)
11. Postskriptum (postscript)

Folgender Brief mag als Beispiel für die heute am häufigsten verwendete Form des Geschäftsbriefs dienen:

---

* British Standards Institution, 2 Park Street, London W1A 2BS.

XYZ Company
PO Box 32901
London EC4T 2VC

Telephone: 0171 429 5000
Telefax: 0171 320 429

letterhead

Your ref:
Our ref: JLS/ue

reference line

3rd July 20..

date

Mr Harald Jaspers
Wein- und Spirituosen GmbH
Eschbachweg 24
D-40625 Düsseldorf

inside address

Dear Mr Jaspers

salutation

Your enquiry of 30 June 20..

subject line

Thank you very much for your recent enquiry about various gin brands, which we read with great interest.

We would be glad to deliver any particular gin you require and are enclosing our latest price list and terms of delivery.

body of the letter

Please let us have your detailed enquiry. If you wish to receive any samples, we can send you a trial pack for your convenience.

We look forward to hearing from you soon.

Yours sincerely

John Smith

J. L. Smith
Sales Manager

complimentary close

name and signature

Encs

enclosures

P.S. We also enclose information about some of our special discounts.

postscript

Die Briefbestandteile

1. Briefkopf (letterhead)

Der Briefkopf ist in der Regel auf dem Briefbogen gedruckt oder er wird bei der Arbeit mit dem Computer in das Schreibprogramm eingespeichert. Der englische Briefkopf muss Namen, Adresse, die Telefon- und Telefaxnummern sowie die E-Mail-Adresse enthalten. Die Namen der Direktoren und die eingetragene Büronummer sind in der Regel ebenfalls zu erwähnen.

2. Bezugszeile (reference line)

Die Bezugszeile besteht gewöhnlich aus den Initialen der Person, die den Brief diktiert hat, und denen der Schreibkraft. Manchmal enthält die Bezugszeile auch ein Geschäftszeichen, das – besonders bei Behörden oder großen Firmen mit zahlreichen Abteilungen – unbedingt in der Antwort angegeben werden sollte.

3. Datum (date)

Die moderne Schreibform für das Datum erlaubt zahlreiche Möglichkeiten, z. B.:

3 July 2010	July 3rd, 2010
3rd July 2010	July 3, 2010
July 3rd 2010	

Man sollte mit Rücksicht auf die anders geartete Schreibweise der Amerikaner vermeiden, nur Zahlen zu schreiben, wie z. B.:

2010-7-3

Diese Schreibform für den 3. Juli 2010 wäre in Amerika durchaus üblich, was natürlich zu Verwechslungen führen könnte. Daher sollte der Monatsname ausgeschrieben bzw., vor allem bei längeren Monatsnamen, in Kurzform genannt werden, z. B.:

3 Feb 2010

Es wird jedoch darauf hingewiesen, dass in vielen Computerprogrammen automatisch das Datum in Zahlen erscheint, z. B.:

2010-07-03

4. Anschrift des Empfängers (inside address)

Beispiele:

Mr J. L. Smith	Miss Rosemary Thunderbell
Mrs A J Gulliver	Messrs Black & Sons
Ms Jane Mason	

Einzelpersonen oder Personengesellschaften werden in der Regel in der oben beschriebenen Weise angeschrieben. "Messrs" steht bei Personengesellschaften nur vor den Namen der Personen, entfällt jedoch, wenn die Personengesellschaft einen Namen hat, der nicht aus Personennamen besteht, z. B.:

The British North Sea Oil Company
The Birmingham Polo Club

Adressiert man den Brief an eine Kapitalgesellschaft, die im Englischen z. B. auf "Ltd" bzw. "Plc" endet, im Amerikanischen häufig auf "Inc.", im Südafrikanischen auf "Pty." usw., schreibt man lediglich den Namen der Firma, z. B.:

The New York Fire Engine Inc.
Robertson & Partners Ltd
Harward & Freytag Plc

5. Anrede (salutation)

Wie Sie eine Person oder Firma anreden, hängt häufig von der Anrede ab, die Sie bei der Empfängeranschrift verwendet haben. "Mr A J Gulliver" würde man folgendermaßen anreden:

Dear Sir   Dear Mr Gulliver

oder, was im Englischen häufig ist, mit Vornamen:

Dear Adam

Bei Damen gilt Ähnliches. "Ms Jane Mason" könnte wie folgt angeredet werden:

Dear Madam
Dear Ms Mason
Dear Jane

Die Abkürzung "Ms" kam ursprünglich aus Amerika, wo Frauen weder ein "Mrs" noch ein "Miss" vor ihren Namen setzen wollten, sondern mit "Ms" lediglich dokumentierten, dass sie weiblichen Geschlechts waren. "Mrs" und "Miss" werden natürlich auch verwendet. Die Abkürzungen "Mr.", "Mrs.", "Ms." werden in amerikanischen Briefen oft mit einem Punkt versehen, in britischen Geschäftsbriefen dagegen nur selten.

Richtet man sich an eine Gesellschaft, in der man noch keine Person mit Namen kennt, schreibt man: "Dear Sirs" oder "Dear Sir or Madam". In den USA findet die Anrede "Gentlemen:" oder "Ladies and Gentlemen:" Verwendung.

Auf Zeichensetzung wird im Zeitalter des Computers in Anschrift und Anrede bei der Blockform (vgl. Briefmuster S. 155) weitgehend verzichtet. Im Brieftext selbst ist sie natürlich nach wie vor von großer Wichtigkeit. Bei amerikanischen Briefen ist die Zeichensetzung dagegen oft in Anrede und Schlussformel zu finden. Die für Geschäftsbriefe eher selten verwendete eingerückte Form verlangt in der Regel die volle Zeichensetzung.

6. Betreff (subject line)

Über die Notwendigkeit eines Betreffs ist man sich innerhalb der verschiedenen Gremien der EU noch nicht einig. Während man in Deutschland offensichtlich noch dazu tendiert, den Betreff als Bestandteil des Briefes aufzufassen, ist er in GB nicht mehr zwingend vorgeschrieben. Obwohl es heißt, dass die Betreffzeile im Englischen <u>nach</u> der der Anrede zu erscheinen hat und nicht <u>vor</u> der Anrede wie im Deutschen, gibt es hiervon auch schon Abweichungen.

7. Brieftext (body of the letter)

Selbst in einem kurzen Geschäftsbrief wird man sich auf drei Teile einigen können: die Einleitung, den eigentlichen Zweck des Briefes und den Schlusssatz.

8. Schlussformel (complimentary close)

Hier gibt es Unterschiede im britischen und amerikanischen Englisch. Während der Brite es sehr genau nimmt, ob er eine Person mit Namen angeredet hat oder nicht, ist der Amerikaner großzügiger.

Schreibt der Brite an eine Person mit Namen, z. B.:

> Dear Thomas
> Dear Mr Smith

muss er in der Schlussformel "Yours sincerely" schreiben.

Schreibt er allgemein:

> Dear Sir
> Dear Madam
> Dear Sir or Madam
> Dear Sirs

heißt die Schlussformel "Yours faithfully".

Wenn man eine Person recht gut kennt, können einige höfliche Floskeln hinzugefügt werden, wie z. B.:

> With best wishes
> Kind regards

In den USA findet man häufig:

> Sincerely yours, oder
> Sincerely,

ganz gleich, wie man die Person vorher angeredet hat.

9. Name und Unterschrift (name and signature)

In GB und den USA unterschreibt den Brief in der Regel die Person, die ihn diktiert oder selbst geschrieben hat. Da Unterschriften häufig unleserlich sind, wird es immer gebräuchlicher, den Namen der Person darunter zu schreiben. Um dem Leser die Stellung der Person, mit der er korrespondiert, zu erläutern, steht häufig auch die Berufsbezeichnung unter dem Namen, z. B.:

> J L Smith
> Sales Manager
>
> Helen Kessler
> Personal Assistant

10. Anlagen (enclosures)

Wenn dem Brief eine Anlage hinzugefügt wird, sollte man dies der Ordnung halber am Schluss des Briefes erwähnen. Dies geschieht normalerweise in Form einer Abkürzung, "encl", "enc(s)".

11. Postskriptum (postscript)

Dieses dient wie im Deutschen dazu, noch etwas unter den Brief zu setzen, was man vergessen hat. Es ist jedoch heute recht selten geworden, da in computergeschriebene Briefe unschwer etwas eingefügt werden kann.

Wichtige Behandlungsvermerke auf Briefen

By airmail	per Luftpost
By registered mail	per Einschreiben
By courier	per Kurier
c/o (care of)	per Adresse, bei
attn (for the attention of)	zu Händen von
Express Delivery	Eilboten
If undelivered, please return	Falls unzustellbar, bitte zurück
To be forwarded } Please forward	Bitte nachsenden
P. O. Box	Post(schließ)fach
Poste restante } To be called for	Postlagernd
Printed matter	Drucksache
Printed matter reduced rate	Drucksache zu ermäßigter Gebühr
Urgent	Eilt
Confidential	Vertraulich
Private and confidential	Streng vertraulich
Private	Privat

Adressen – Die britischen und amerikanischen Postzustellsysteme – Die Postleitzahlen

In Großbritannien gibt es noch immer zwei Postzustellsysteme "first class post", etwa Postzustelldienst 1. Klasse, und "second class post", etwa Postzustelldienst 2. Klasse, welcher billiger, aber auch langsamer ist.

Jede Adresse in Großbritannien hat einen "postcode", eine Postleitzahl, die aus jeweils zwei Gruppen von Buchstaben und Zahlen besteht. Die erste Gruppe zeigt an, in welche Stadt oder ihre Umgebung der Adressat postalisch einzuordnen ist. Die zweite Gruppe gibt genauen Aufschluss über die Adresse innerhalb dieses Wohngebiets.

Da Maschinen diese Zahlen- und Buchstabengruppen noch nicht erfassen können, werden sie von Postbediensteten als "blue dots" (blaue Punkte) auf die Umschläge getippt. Diese können von elektronischen Sortiermaschinen mit einer Geschwindigkeit von 16 000 Stück pro Stunde gelesen und sortiert werden.

Eine richtig geschriebene Adresse sollte wie folgt aussehen:

Ms Anne Howard
16 Garden Avenue
HARWICH
CO12 4JR
England

Die Länderbezeichnung ist nur erforderlich, wenn der Brief außerhalb von Großbritannien abgeschickt wird.

Die Namen der wichtigsten postalisch anerkannten Abkürzungen für Grafschaften, die jedoch nicht mehr verbindlich in den Adressen angegeben werden müssen, lauten wie folgt:

Bedfordshire	Beds	Northamptonshire	Northants
Berkshire	Berks	Northumberland	Northd
Buckinghamshire	Bucks	Nottinghamshire	Notts
Cambridgeshire	Cambs	Oxfordshire	Oxon
Gloucestershire	Glos	Shropshire	Shrops/Salop
Hampshire	Hants	South Glamorgan	S Glam
Hertfordshire	Herts	Staffordshire	Staffs
Lancashire	Lancs	West Glamorgan	W Glam
Leicestershire	Leics	Wiltshire	Wilts
Lincolnshire	Lincs	Worcestershire	Worcs
Mid Glamorgan	M Glam	Yorkshire	Yorks
Middlesex	Middx		

Bei der Adressierung ist es in den USA wichtig, die Abkürzung für den jeweiligen Staat in zwei Großbuchstaben sowie die Postleitzahl (die im amerikanischen Englisch "ZIP code" heißt) anzugeben.

In den Vereinigten Staaten ist es üblich, die Adresse in Großbuchstaben und ohne Zeichensetzung auf den Umschlag zu schreiben, z. B.:

MS ANNE SMITH
57 MAIN DRIVE
ORLANDO, FL 935281
USA

Die Namen der US-Staaten und deren Gebiete mit Abkürzungen lauten wie folgt:

Alabama	AL	Kentucky	KY	Oklahoma	OK
Alaska	AK	Louisiana	LA	Oregon	OR
Arizona	AZ	Maine	ME	Pennsylvania	PA
Arkansas	AR	Maryland	MD	Puerto Rico	PR
California	CA	Massachusetts	MA	Rhode Island	RI
Colorado	CO	Michigan	MI	South Carolina	SC
Connecticut	CT	Minnesota	MN	South Dakota	SD
Delaware	DE	Mississippi	MS	Tennessee	TN
District of		Missouri	MO	Texas	TX
Columbia	DC	Montana	MT	Utah	UT
Florida	FL	Nebraska	NE	Vermont	VT
Georgia	GA	Nevada	NV	Virginia	VA
Guam	GU	New Hampshire	NH	Virgin Islands	VI
Hawaii	HI	New Jersey	NJ	Washington	WA
Idaho	ID	New Mexico	NM	West Virginia	WV
Illinois	IL	New York	NY	Wisconsin	WI
Indiana	IN	North Carolina	NC	Wyoming	WY
Iowa	IA	North Dakota	ND		
Kansas	KS	Ohio	OH		

Muster für richtig adressierte Briefumschläge befinden sich auf S. 158.

Das Telefax und die E-Mail

In einer Zeit ständig steigender Kommunikationsmöglichkeiten und immer schneller schriftlicher Nachrichtenübermittlungswege haben sich das Telefax und die E-Mail einen nicht mehr wegzudenkenden Platz erobert und das Fernschreiben weitestgehend verdrängt.

Telefaxe sind geschäftsbriefähnliche, jedoch meist weniger formgebundene schriftliche Nachrichten, die über getrennte Faxgeräte, die telefonisch anwählbar sind, oder auch computergesteuert direkt vom Absender an den Empfänger geschickt werden können.

E-Mails (electronic mail) werden in formloser oder auch geschäftsbriefähnlicher Form über das Internet versandt. Hierfür verwendet man sogenannte E-Mail-Adressen, die bei Providern eingerichtet werden. Das Internet erlaubt den schnellen und kostengünstigen Versand von Nachrichten und Daten jeglicher Art und Größe weltweit. Dies schafft für E-Mails praktisch unbegrenzte Möglichkeiten der Kommunikation und wird in Zukunft in diesem Bereich für eine revolutionäre Entwicklung sorgen.

FAX MESSAGE

To: Ms Lydia Haverkamp
Fax No.   +49(0)211 535553
From: John Smith
Fax No.   +44(0)171 2804025
Date: 21 Aug 20..
Pages: 1

Dear Lydia

This is to confirm that I sent you the required documents yesterday.

Best regards
John Smith

---

e-mail

From:	Peter.Schwabe@webside.de
To:	John.Warnock@abtal.com
Date:	15 Oct 20..
Subject:	Your information of 14 Oct 20..

Dear John:

Thank you for your mail dated 24 March 20.. and file attachments. The figures stated are fine and may be submitted to the Ontario tax authorities.

Regards,
Peter Schwabe

Es gibt bisher weder für das Fax noch für die E-Mail feste Normen. Beim Fax werden in der Regel zumindest Absender und Empfänger und die entsprechenden Fax-Nummern erwähnt, bei der E-Mail erscheinen Absender- und Empfängeradressen automatisch; ein wichtiges Element ist die Angabe des Betreffs, die dem Empfänger die Entscheidung erleichtert, ob und wann er die E-Mail-Nachricht öffnen soll.

Britisches und amerikanisches Englisch

Die Unterschiede zwischen britischem und amerikanischem Englisch, die für die schriftliche Geschäftskommunikation relevant sind, sind nicht so ausgeprägt wie in der Umgangssprache oder in anderen Bereichen. Detaillierte Auskunft hierüber gibt ein gutes einsprachiges Wörterbuch, wie z. b. das *Dictionary of English Language and Culture*, Longman. Zwei Aspekte sind aber für das Schreiben von Briefen im Allgemeinen wichtig, nämlich die Unterschiede in der Rechtschreibung und im Wortschatz.

Rechtschreibung

Gegenüber dem britischen Englisch (BE) weist die Rechtschreibung im amerikanischen Englisch (AE) hauptsächlich folgende Eigenheiten auf:

1. Häufige Weglassung des Bindestrichs, z. B. *newsstand, breakdown, soapbox, cooperate*. Viele dieser Weglassungen finden zunehmend im BE Verbreitung.

2. Viele Wörter, die im BE auf **-our** enden, enden im amerikanischen Englisch auf **-or**, z. B.: *color, humor, favor, honor.*

3. Viele Wörter, die im BE auf **-re** enden, enden im AE auf **-er**, z. B.: *theater, center, fiber*. Ausnahme: *massacre.*

4. Viele Wörter, die im BE auf **-gue** enden, lassen das **-ue** im AE weg, z. B.: *catalog, dialog.*

5. Viele Wörter, die im BE auf **-ce** enden, enden im AE auf **-se**, z. B.: *license, defense, practise* (im AE auch im Substantiv).

6. Wortstämme, die im BE auf **-l** enden, verdoppeln dieses, wenn die Endsilbe mit einem Vokal beginnt. Im AE entfällt das zweite **-l**, z. B.: *dial* – BE *dialled*, AE *dialed, travel* – BE *travelled*, AE *traveled.*

7. Stummes **-e-** entfällt im AE in Wörtern wie: *abridg(e)ment, judg(e)ment, acknowledg(e)ment.*

8. Neben *although, all right, through* finden sich die informell-familiären Formen *altho, alright, thru.*

9. Weitere Unterschiede in der Schreibweise gibt es bei Wörtern, wie z. B.:

BE	AE
tyre	tire
cheque	check
aluminium	aluminum

Wortschatz

Im Laufe der Zeit haben sich in den USA vom BE abweichende Bezeichnungen durchgesetzt, wie z. B.:

BE	AE
autumn	fall
underground, tube	subway
motorway	highway, freeway, interstate
queue	line
petrol (station)	gas (station)
flyover	overpass
flat	apartment
ground floor	first floor
first floor	second floor
lift	elevator
pavement	sidewalk
rates	property tax
timetable	schedule
toilet	bathroom, restroom
company	corporation
public limited company	stock corporation

Silbentrennung

Im Gegensatz zum Deutschen werden englische Wörter nicht immer streng nach Silben getrennt, es gilt aber schon der Grundsatz, dass nur zwei- oder mehrsilbige Wörter überhaupt getrennt werden dürfen. Wörter wie z.B. "asked" oder "called" werden nicht getrennt.

Im Allgemeinen hat das Prinzip der Erkennbarkeit des jeweiligen Wortes oder Wortteils Vorrang, um dem Leser zu ermöglichen, das Wort richtig auszusprechen. Das Wort "listen" kann z.B. nur zwischen "s" und "t" getrennt werden: "lis-ten", weil eine Trennung hinter dem "t" den Leser dazu verleiten würde, das Wort falsch mit hörbarem "t" auszusprechen, d. h. "list-" gefolgt von "-en". Ähnliche Beispiele sind "coach-ing" (nicht "co-ach-ing") und "coin-age" (nicht "co-inage"). Ein weiteres Beispiel wäre auch "'pho-to-graph" und "pho-'tog-ra-pher". Wörter mit gleicher Schreibung, aber anderer Lautung wie "(a) 'present" und "(to) pre'sent" müssen auch entsprechend der Regel der Erkennbarkeit getrennt werden, und zwar "(a) 'pres-ent" und "(to) pre-'sent".

Des Weiteren ist es normalerweise nicht zulässig, ein Wort so zu trennen, dass nur zwei Buchstaben am Anfang der zweiten Zeile erscheinen (z.B. vor der "-ed"-Endung). Zwei Buchstaben am Ende der ersten Zeile sind zwar möglich (z.B. re-produce), aber nicht wünschenswert.

Vorsilben wie "ante-" oder "anti-" werden nicht getrennt. Doppelbuchstaben werden getrennt (z.B. al-low, dis-solve, con-nect, as-sume, in-nocu-ous), es sei denn, dass eine Trennung die Bestandteile des Wortes irreführend darstellt (z.B. inn-keep-er, call-ing, pass-ing).

Interpunktion

Der Apostroph

Ein Apostroph kann besitzanzeigend gebraucht werden: "The Manager's car is outside", "The managers' cars are outside", oder es ersetzt einen fehlenden Buchstaben: "The Manager's here." (d.h. "The Manager is here.").

In seltenen Fällen kann die Mehrzahl mit Apostroph-s gebildet werden, und zwar bei Zahlen: "the 70's and the 80's" (wobei die Schreibweise ohne Apostroph als akzeptabel gilt: "the 70s and the 80s"), oder bei Wörtern, die normalerweise keine Mehrzahl besitzen: "too many if's and but's".

Das Komma

Das Komma ist nur in seltenen Fällen ein streng vorgeschriebenes Satzzeichen. Nebensätze werden nicht immer vom Hauptsatz durch ein Komma getrennt, und zwar vor allem nicht bei Objektsätzen (z.B. "He knows that I'm English."). Bei "if"-Sätzen wird bei kürzeren Sätzen das Komma oft weggelassen, bei längeren Sätzen dagegen zur besseren Überschaubarkeit gesetzt:

> Call me if he comes.

> If the Managing Director asks me to contact him, I'd like you to leave
> a message with my secretary.

Ein Komma symbolisiert oft eine Sprechpause. Demzufolge erscheint es dort, wo der Sprecher kurz innehalten würde, z. B. vor und nach "however", "nevertheless", "strangely enough" usw.

Kommas werden benutzt, um einen nicht notwendigen Relativsatz vom Hauptsatz zu trennen: "My brother John, who lives in London, is here." Notwendige Relativsätze werden vom Hauptsatz nicht durch Kommas getrennt: "The man who came yesterday is here again."

Groß- und Kleinschreibung

In englischen Geschäftsbriefen gelten die sonst üblichen Regeln der Groß- und Kleinschreibung der englischen Sprache, aber zur Hervorhebung wichtiger Wörter in der Handelskorrespondenz, wie z.B. Bill of Lading, Certificate of Origin, Commercial Invoice usw., können große Anfangsbuchstaben verwendet werden.

Wenn auf die Titel von Mitarbeitern einer Firma, die bestimmte Positionen innehaben, Bezug genommen wird, ist ein großer Anfangsbuchstabe erforderlich: "The Manager has instructed the Finance Controller to redraft the Commercial Invoice."

Einfache Anfrage
Simple enquiry

25 November 20..

Clearcut Lawnmowers Ltd
90–100 Clover Drive
TORRINGTON
Kent
TZ3 8ZZ
United Kingdom

Dear Sirs

We are a newly-established firm specializing in the supply of gardening equipment. As we are currently in the process of buying in stock in good time for the coming spring season, we would be grateful if you would send us a catalogue of your full lawnmower range, both mechanical and electric.

Would you also indicate how much time should be allowed for delivery and include details of your export prices and quantity discounts. Please also state whether goods on a sale or return basis can be supplied and what your position on after-sales service is.

If your products are to good standard and delivery is prompt, we feel sure that there will be ample opportunity for your company to acquire a substantial share of the market here.

Yours faithfully
Brill Gartengeräte GmbH

Thomas Wolf
Assistant Manager

newly-established neu gegründet
gardening equipment Gartengerät
buy in stock Lagervorräte einkaufen
lawnmower Rasenmäher
range Serie, Palette
export price Exportpreis
quantity discount Mengenrabatt
sale or return Kauf mit Rückgaberecht
after-sales service Kundendienst
be to good standard einem guten Standard entsprechen
ample opportunity reichlich Gelegenheit
share of the market Marktanteil

2 Anfrage
Enquiry

February 28, 20..

Computronic Inc
PO Box 8732
Austin, TX 75110
USA

Ladies and Gentlemen:

ENCRYPTION SOFTWARE

We read your advertisement in the latest edition of DataNews, in which you state that you have developed new software for the encryption of electronic data.

We are in the process of reviewing our company's security procedures and wish to introduce a hierarchical system of data access using unbreakable passwords.

We would be most interested in receiving a demonstration version of your encryption program, which we would then attempt to crack. If, using a powerful mainframe computer, we do not succeed, we will place a substantial order for your software.

We look forward to receiving your comments on this matter, together with details of on-site after-sales service and up-date facilities, should you feel that your product will pass the test we intend it to undergo.

Yours truly,
BOCHUMER DATENTECHNIK

Reinhardt Deutsch
Software Engineer

encryption
  Verschlüsselung, Kodierung
electronic data
  elektronische Daten
security procedure
  Sicherheitsverfahren
data access
  Datenzugang
unbreakable passwords
  unaufschlüsselbare Kennwörter
demonstration version
  Vorführversion
crack knacken
mainframe computer
  Großrechner
comments
  Stellungnahme
on-site
  an Ort und Stelle
after-sales service
  Kundendienst
up-date
  auf den neuesten Stand bringen

TELEFAX

23 March 20..

TO: POLISH CHAMBER OF COMMERCE
FAX: +4822 274673

FROM: BILL JAMBOR, Lancashire Enterprises plc
FAX: +1773 721029

Dear Sirs

My company is at present tendering for an EC project in Romania. I would be pleased if you could send me details of Polish companies able to supply the following equipment:

1. Engine compressor spare parts, engine spare parts and pistons for Ikarus motor vehicles, Types 260.50, 280.33, 280.64

2. Spare parts for "Tatra" Trams, type T4R

3. Electrolyte copper cathode and 18mm diameter copper winding wire

4. Equipment and spare parts for diesel electric and electric locomotives

5. Rail coach batteries, locomotive starter batteries and locomotive storage batteries

The exact details and conditions of tender will be sent to the relevant companies.

We unfortunately have very little time to submit our tender and would thus be grateful to receive details from you as soon as possible and in any event in no later than two weeks from now.

Yours faithfully
...

tender   (formell)
anbieten, sich an einer Ausschreibung beteiligen
compressor
Kompressor
engine spare part
Maschinenersatzteil
piston   Kolben
electrolyte
Elektrolyt
copper cathode
Kupferkathode
winding wire
Wickeldraht
rail coach battery
Eisenbahnwaggonbatterie
starter battery
Starterbatterie
storage battery
Speicherbatterie
submit
unterbreiten

21

4 Anfrage aufgrund einer Anzeige
Enquiry in response to an advertisement

From: jackson&partners@tel.com.uk
To: m.prinzen@liberty.de
Date: 22 March 20..
Subject: Request for sales literature

For the attention of Monika Prinzen

Dear Ms Prinzen

LADIES' SUMMER WEAR

We refer to your advertisement in this month's edition of "Fashion Plus".

We are a major importer of ladies' fashion wear with a network of retail outlets throughout the UK. For the past 10 years we have, with considerable success, been dealing in fashions for teenagers and the early 20s. Our lines are strictly up-market and are always in instant response to current trends.

Please send us your catalogue, a current export price-list including terms of payment and delivery and details of quantity discounts. We would also appreciate it if you would include representative samples of some of this season's garments to enable us to assess their quality.

We feel sure that there could be considerable openings for competitively priced goods of the right design and look forward to hearing from you in good time for the coming season.

Postal address:
Jackson & Partners Ltd.
P.O. Box 11058, LONDON, SW1 3YK, U.K.

Yours sincerely
Jackson & Partners Ltd.
...

major importer
größerer Importeur
retail outlet
Einzelhandelsverkaufsstelle
the early 20s
Leute Anfang 20
line *hier:* Stil, Kollektion
be strictly up-market *hier:* den höchsten Ansprüchen genügen
be in instant response *hier:* sofort reagieren
current trend
aktueller Trend
export price-list
Exportpreisliste
quantity discount
Mengenrabatt
openings *hier:* Chancen, Möglichkeiten
competitively priced goods
Waren zu konkurrenzfähigen Preisen

Lancashire Enterprises plc
Enterprise House
17 Ribblesdale Place
Winckley Square
Preston PR7 3NA

Genesis Medical Ltd
115 Gloucester Road
LONDON
SW 7 3WW

12 December 20..

Dear Sirs

SINGLE USE TRANSFUSION SET

We were given your name by our mutual business associate, Neil Smith at Medical Systems (International) Ltd, who recommended that we contact you.

Lancashire Enterprises plc is actively involved in eastern Europe, having won major contracts to help revitalise the industrial base of countries effecting the transition to a market economy. Included in this work is the provision of a trading service.

In this respect we have been approached by a Polish manufacturer of Single Use Transfusion Sets (sample enclosed), who has requested us to seek business contacts in western Europe on his behalf.

As sole UK agents for the manufacturer, we are able to supply you the sets at a CIF unit price of £ ... . We are able to supply 8500 units per shipment and up to three shipments per month.

The manufacturing process used conforms to international standards. The manufacturer is in the process of applying for the Department of Health certificate and would welcome an order subject to obtaining such certification.

.../2

single use transfusion set Einwegbesteck für Transfusionen
business associate Geschäftspartner
win major contracts den Zuschlag für größere Aufträge erhalten
revitalise wieder beleben
effect the transition to den Übergang zu ... verwirklichen
market economy Marktwirtschaft
provision *hier:* Bereitstellung
seek business contacts Geschäftskontakte suchen
sole agent Alleinvertreter
manufacturing process Herstellungsverfahren
international standards internationale Normen

In addition, if a good response from UK firms is forthcoming, the packaging will be modified and the instructions will be printed in English.

Furthermore, should you so require, the product can be modified to suit individual requirements.

We look forward to your response and would welcome an opportunity to strengthen ties with eastern Europe. We also enclose for your information a brochure describing our activities in this field in more detail.

Yours faithfully
Lancashire Enterprises plc

Bill Jambor
Project Executive

Enc

Department of Health
(brit.) Gesundheitsministerium
subject to
sofern, ... unter der Bedingung, dass
be forthcoming
sich einstellen, erfolgen
suit individual requirements
individuellen Bedürfnissen entsprechen
strengthen ties with
Bindungen mit ... stärken

June 20..

Schulz Import- und Export
Handelsgesellschaft mbH
Kurfürstenstr. 20
90459 Nürnberg
GERMANY

Gentlemen:

Subject: Door-to-Door Delivery

Don't throw this letter away! It's worth real money to anybody who'll give us a chance to prove just how good we are!

Why worry about keeping to those delivery dates stipulated in your Sales Contract using the regular, state-owned mail service when you can make use of a custom-made personalized, door-to-door delivery service right now! We have a fleet of trucks near your town and, likely as not, based near your block, just waiting to rush your goods to their destinations.

We have already made ourselves into a household name in the US and now, by popular request, we have extended our operation to Europe, East and West. We can provide transportation for anything from a string of pearls to a pipeline – to any destination you care to name. Just call us on a local low-toll number and we'll quote you right away. We specialize in rock-bottom priced, just-in-time delivery with full insurance cover.

We're waiting to hear from you. Just pick up that phone and call us – you'll never look back!

Sincerely yours,
…

stipulate
festsetzen
state-owned mail service
staatliches Postzu-stellungssystem
custom-made
nach Kundenan-gaben erstellt
door-to-door delivery service
Zustelldienst von Haus zu Haus
fleet of trucks
Lkw-Fuhrpark
household name
bekannter Name
string of pearls
Perlenschnur
low-toll number
Nummer zu nied-riger (Fernsprech-) Gebühr
rock-bottom price
niedrigst kalkulier-ter Preis
full insurance cover
volle Versiche-rungsdeckung

7 Verlangtes Angebot
Solicited offer

May 21, 20..

Ex- und Import Industriegüter
Handelsgesellschaft mbH
Kernerplatz 4
70182 Stuttgart
GERMANY

Attn. Mr. Rolf Stein

Dear Mr. Stein,

Many thanks for your enquiry of May 10 regarding the importation of our new, environmentally friendly, CFC-free packaging material.

We will have no difficulty in manufacturing and supplying the shapes you describe in the drawings included with your enquiry, since we have a molding technique which enables us to customize packaging to customers' specifications. So far, we have had an overwhelming response from all over the world to our new product and our production department is being expanded to cope with the increasing demand.

We enclose our catalog and current export price-list. All prices are exclusive of tax and are quoted FCA US airport. At present, delivery to a US airport can be made within 3–4 weeks of receipt of order. We look forward to executing your order and enclose our Order Form for customer convenience.

Sincerely yours,
...

environmentally friendly umweltfreundlich
CFC-free = chlorofluorocarbon-free FCKW-frei = frei von Fluorchlorkohlenwasserstoffen
packaging material Verpackungsmaterial
molding technique Formtechnik
customize auf den Kundenbedarf zuschneiden
catalog Katalog
exclusive of tax ohne Steuer
FCA = Free Carrier *(Incoterm)*
order form Auftragsformular
for customer convenience für die Bequemlichkeit des Kunden

7 December 20..

Turnpike Traders Ltd
Units 1–4
Greenman Industrial Estate
BLACKBURN
BB1 5QF

Dear Sirs

This morning we took delivery of the 50 boards of prime quality teak ordered as per our letter of 1 November (Order No. WW-T1-11).

The quality of 2 of the boards is, however, unsatisfactory as they contain large, unsightly knots rendering them unsuitable for use.

We feel sure that this is an oversight on your part but, owing to the considerable number of orders in hand, we had no alternative but to return the goods in question to you, carriage forward, on the assumption that you will arrange for replacements to be sent to us by return to enable us to keep to production schedules.

We trust that you will be in agreement with this course of action and look forward to receiving replacements corresponding to your otherwise high standards.

Yours faithfully
WELLING & BURBURY LIMITED

William Welling
Chief Executive

prime quality teak erstklassiges Teakholz
unsatisfactory nicht zufrieden stellend
unsightly unansehnlich, hässlich
unsuitable for use unbenutzbar
oversight Versehen
order in hand vorliegender Auftrag
carriage forward unfrei, Fracht vom Empfänger zu zahlen
by return umgehend
keep to *hier:* einhalten
production schedule Produktionsplan
be in agreement with einverstanden sein mit
high standard hohes Niveau, gute Qualität

9 Berichtigung einer Reklamation
Adjustment of a claim

March 26, 20..

Magnetische Informations- und Datensysteme
Gewerbepark
59069 Hamm
GERMANY

Attn: Mr. Andreas Schulz

Dear Mr. Schulz:

Subject: Complaint re DRT/398 Semi-conductors

Thank you for your communication of March 10, in which you state that the semi-conductors supplied are not up to standard.

Having looked into the matter we are now able to tell you that you were mistakenly supplied with DRT/298 semi-conductors, which, despite having similar properties to the latest version, are not able to perform as consistently as their successor.

We apologize for the inconvenience caused and would suggest that we either take back the consignment, carriage forward with insurance covered by us and replace it by DRT/398s, or reduce the price of the goods you have received to the standard list-price, with a further discount of 10% to make up for the inconvenience caused.

Please fax us your reply at your earliest convenience. Should you opt for a replacement delivery we will rush the goods to you by airmail.

Sincerely yours,
...

semiconductor
Halbleiter
be up to standard
dem (normalen) Standard entsprechen
look into the matter
die Sache untersuchen
be mistakenly supplied
fälschlicherweise beliefert werden
similar property
ähnliche Eigenschaft
consistently
gleichmäßig, zuverlässig
inconvenience
Unannehmlichkeit
with insurance covered by us
Versicherungsdeckung durch uns
make up for
entschädigen für
opt for
sich entscheiden für
replacement delivery
Ersatzlieferung

15 February 20..

Benson Bank plc
42 Leadenhall Street
LONDON
EC1 7HJ

Dear Sir or Madam

A. P. Jones & Sons Limited
Account Number 28625309

The above-mentioned customer has approached us requesting a credit facility amounting to £15,000 per month on 30-day terms.

We would be most grateful if you would advise us whether the company in question is sufficiently sound for such a facility.

Should you so prefer, please feel free to reply via our bankers, SouthWest plc, Hounslow Bath Road Branch, Middlesex MX1 4WW quoting our account number 29560277.

Any information given will, of course, be treated in the strictest confidence with no obligation on your part.

Yours faithfully
INTERFORM LTD

P. J. Smith
Managing Director

approach s.o.
sich an j-n wenden
credit facility
Kreditmöglichkeit,
Kreditbetrag
on 30-day terms
mit 30-tägiger
Laufzeit
advise
hier: mitteilen
sufficiently
ausreichend
sound
solide, gesund
via über, durch
our bankers
unsere Bank(ver-
bindung)
account number
Kontonummer
**in the strictest con-
fidence**
streng vertraulich
**with no obligation
on your part**
für Sie unverbind-
lich

11 Negative Bankauskunft
Unfavourable bank reference

28 February 20..

Charles Cape & Co Ltd
42 New Fetter Lane
LONDON
EC1A 4WW

Dear Sirs

Easifit Car Accessories Limited

In response to your request for a reference regarding the above-mentioned firm, we must point out that the firm in question has not been known to us for long.

We are thus unable to furnish you with the information you require.

We regret not being in a position to assist you in this matter.

Yours faithfully
NorthEast Bank plc

T. B. Smith
Assistant Manager
Corporate Accounts Dept.

accessory
  Zubehör(teil)
in response to
  als Antwort auf
point out
  hinweisen auf
firm in question
  fragliche Firma
furnish s.o. with s. th.
  j-n mit etw. beliefern, j-m etw. geben
be in a position
  in der Lage sein
Corporate Accounts Dept.
  Abteilung für Geschäftskunden

March 31, 20..

IGI Gesellschaft für Handel,
Export und Import
Schwanallee 135
35037 Marburg
Germany

STRICTLY CONFIDENTIAL

Ladies and Gentlemen:

Thank you for enquiry regarding the company you refer to in your letter of March 15.

Due to the fact that we have only held the subject's account for some six months now we are not able to assist you in this matter.

We regret not being able to help you this time.

Sincerely yours,

Thomas G. Slade
Business Accounts Division

due to the fact that
  aufgrund der
  Tatsache, dass
hold an account
  ein Konto führen
subject
  hier: Kunde, Firma
assist   helfen
**Business Accounts
  Division**
  Geschäftskonten-
  abteilung, Abteilung
  für Geschäftskun-
  den

13 Bitte um Kreditauskunft
Request for a credit reference

➡ Brief 14

Funke-Kaiser GmbH
Nordstraße 24
47169 Duisburg
Germany

U2/45
23 July 20..

Hamlyn Engineering
Golden Crescent
HAYES
MX1 UB3
England

PRIVATE AND CONFIDENTIAL

Dear Sirs

We have recently been approached by the firm mentioned on the enclosed slip, who have requested us to grant them a credit facility amounting to € 5,000 per quarter. We understand from the firm in question that you have been dealing with them for some time and they have suggested that we request you to supply an appropriate trade reference.

We would be grateful if you would kindly reply to the following questions to enable us to conclude whether the business of subject is sufficiently sound to support the facility mentioned. Your early response using the stamped addressed envelope enclosed would be much appreciated.

1. How long has subject been known to you?
2. What amount of credit facility do you normally allow subject?
3. On what terms do you trade with subject?

...../2

private and confidential streng vertraulich
slip Blatt, Zettel
credit facility Kreditrahmen
per quarter vierteljährlich
appropriate geeignet, angemessen
trade reference Handelsauskunft
business of subject *hier:* die infrage stehende Firma
sound solide, gesund
support *hier:* verdienen
addressed envelope adressierter Umschlag
subject *hier:* die betreffende Firma

4. Are payments made promptly / slowly / very slowly?
5. Have you ever had occasion to threaten to take legal proceedings to recover sums due to you?
6. Please also give any other information you feel is relevant.

We assure you that any information given will be treated in the strictest confidence. Please do not hesitate to contact us in future should you require us to reciprocate.

Yours faithfully
FUNKE-KAISER GmbH

Johannes Schmitt
Managing Director

Enc

take legal proceedings
gerichtliche Schritte unternehmen
recover sums
Summen eintreiben
due to s. o.
fällig an j-n
relevant
wichtig, bedeutend
treat behandeln
reciprocate
hier: einen Gegendienst erweisen

14 Positive Kreditauskunft einer Firma
Favourable credit reference from a firm

➡ Brief 13

30 July 20..

Funke-Kaiser GmbH
Nordstraße 24
47169 Duisburg
Germany

CONFIDENTIAL

Dear Mr. Schmitt

In response to your letter dated 23 July 19..,
ref. No.U2/45, we are pleased to supply you with
the following information.

The firm in question are well established on the
local market and have a good reputation. As far as
we know they have been trading for over 15 years
in our field of enterprise and have built up a sizeable network of overseas customers.

We have been dealing with them for the past
8 years now on quarterly account terms and are
pleased to report that they have always met their
financial commitments punctually and in full.
We have, thus far, extended them a credit line of
up to € 2,500 in any given quarter but would have
no hesitation in increasing it to double this figure,
should the need arise.

We trust that this information will be of use to
you and would point out that it is given in the strictest confidence with no obligation whatsoever on
our part.

Yours sincerely
HAMLYN ENGINEERING

Harry Hamlyn
Chief Executive

field of enterprise
  Unternehmens-
  bereich
sizeable
  (ziemlich) groß,
  beträchtlich
overseas
  (von GB aus): aus-
  ländisch
  sonst: überseeisch
**on quarterly ac-
  count terms**
  mit vierteljährli-
  chem Zahlungsziel
**meet one's financial
  commitments**
  seinen finanziellen
  Verpflichtungen
  nachkommen
extend
  hier: gewähren
credit line
  Kreditlinie
**in any given
  quarter**   in jedem
  beliebigen Quartal
on our part
  unsererseits

28 April 20..

Coupre Links 401
9000 GENT
Belgium

Fax: 00 32 56 773058

Dear Sir or Madam

RE: SOURCING GINSENG ROOTS

With reference to our fax of 22 April please note that our contacts in China have just confirmed that small samples and descriptive literature have been despatched. As soon as we receive this material we will pass it on to you.

The price CIF Antwerp is generally something in the region of US$ 25 per kg - types, quality, minimum order quantity, delivery etc. to be confirmed.

In the meantime we would appreciate some information on your company's background and financial standing. We would point out at this juncture that it is to be expected that the Chinese supplier will stipulate payment by letter of credit.

Should you have any queries please do not hesitate to contact us.

Yours faithfully
Lancashire Enterprises plc

Mannix Fu
Project Executive / Trade Dept.

source Bezugsquelle finden
root Wurzel
sample Muster
descriptive literature Informationsmaterial
despatch schicken, (ver-)senden
be something in the region of sich etwa bewegen um
minimum order quantity Mindestbestellmenge
financial standing finanzielle Lage
at this juncture an dieser Stelle, in diesem Augenblick
stipulate festsetzen
payment by letter of credit Zahlung per Akkreditiv
trade dept Handelsabteilung

18 February 20..

Prince DIY Centre
75 – 95 New Hall Street
OXFORD
OX1 7HH

Dear Customer

DIY ON YOUR DOORSTEP!

We are delighted to report that customer demand for our unbeaten range of "do-it-yourself" equipment and materials has increased at such a staggering pace, that we are shortly to be opening a second branch just outside town on the new Pricewise Trading Estate.

Our new branch, at 42 – 50 Grove Road, will provide ample parking facilities and will stock all the lines you have come to know and rely on together with a whole new range of modestly priced accessories for the DIY-enthusiast working on his own. This range will include "one-hand" tools enabling the handiman (or woman!) to manipulate equipment with one hand only, leaving the other free.

Just to convince you how serious we are, we're offering a 5% discount on all cash sales over £25 during the first month of business as from the first of next month. We'll deliver all bulky items (marked with a red star on the price tag) to your front door absolutely free of charge within a 25-mile radius.

So don't miss the chance of cashing in on our once-in-a-lifetime throw-away offers! We're looking forward to greeting you on our new premises on June 1st and we're absolutely certain you'll be glad you came!

Yours sincerely
...

at a staggering pace
in einem Schwindel erregenden Tempo
parking facilities
Parkmöglichkeiten
modestly priced accessories
Zubehörteile zu bescheidenen Preisen
"one-hand" tool
Werkzeug, das mit einer Hand bedient werden kann
handiman
hier: Heimwerker
cash sale
Barverkauf
bulky   groß, sperrig
price tag
Preisschild
within a 25-mile radius
in einem Umkreis von 25 Meilen
miss the chance
die Gelegenheit verpassen
once-in-a-lifetime
einmal im Leben vorkommend
a throw-away offer
hier: ein einmalig preiswertes Angebot

12 September 20..

Torrington Marine Co Ltd
Unit 8
Greenway Industrial Estate
BLACKBURN
BA3 8IJ

Dear Sirs

We have been requested by the Bank of International Commerce in the Sultanate of Oman to advise the issue of their irrevocable Credit Number 344912/92 in your favour for account of

MidEast Marine

of Kuwi, Sultanate of Oman, P.O. Box 61842, for £25,000 (SAY TWENTY-FIVE THOUSAND POUNDS STERLING) available by your drafts on us at 30 days sight accompanied by the following documents:

1. Signed invoices in triplicate certifying goods are in accordance with order No. 2092/92 dated 15 August 20.. between MidEast Marine and Torrington Marine Co Ltd.

2. Marine and War Risk Insurance Certificate covering "All risks" warehouse to warehouse, for 10% above the CIF value, evidencing that claims are payable in the Sultanate of Oman.

3. Complete set 3/3 Shipping Company's clean "on board" ocean Bills of Lading made out to order of the shippers and endorsed to order of the Bank of International Commerce, Sultanate of Oman,

...../2

for account of
auf Rechnung von
draft on us
auf uns gezogener Wechsel
at 30 days sight
auf 30 Tage Sicht
in triplicate
dreifach
marine and war risk insurance certificate
Versicherungszertifikat zur Abdeckung des See- und Kriegsrisikos
all risks
alle Risiken
clean "on board" ocean bill of lading
reines "an Bord" Seekonnossement
made out to order
an Order lautend
endorse
indossieren
freight paid
Fracht bezahlt

marked "Freight Paid" and "Notify MidEast Marine of Kuwi, Sultanate of Oman, P.O. Box 61842".

Covering: 3x Type 500-D Outboard Motors CIF Muscat
Shipped from UK Port to Muscat
Partshipment prohibited
Transhipment prohibited
Documents must be presented for payment within 15 days from the date of shipment.

We are requested to add our confirmation to this Credit and we hereby undertake to pay you the face amount of your drafts drawn within its terms, provided such drafts bear the number and date of the Credit and that the Letter of Credit and all amendments thereto are attached.

The Credit is subject to Uniform Customs and Practices for Documentary Credits (1983 Revision), International Chamber of Commerce Publication No. 400.

Drafts shown under this Credit must be presented to us for payment / negotiation / acceptance not later than 12 October 20.. and marked "Drawn under Credit Number 344912/92" of the Bank of International Commerce Sultanate of Oman.

Dated ...

Signed ...

p.p.
York Bank plc
91 Mosley Street
Manchester MA1 3UZ

---

outboard motor
  Außenbordmotor
partshipment
  Teilverschiffung
transhipment
  Umladung
undertake
  sich verpflichten
face amount
  Nennwert
amendment
  Änderung
attach
  beifügen
be subject to
  unterliegen
uniform
  einheitlich
negotiation
  hier: Begebung
acceptance
  Akzept

Vergabe eines bestimmten Auftrages
Placing a specific order

➡ Briefe 19–22

17 October 20..

Lupton Bros Ltd
P.O. Box 8
Fountain Works
Portland Street
ACCRINGTON
BB5 1RJ
England

Dear Sirs

OUR PURCHASE ORDER NO.5769F/KED

We refer to your fax No. 0254 36279 dated 5 October 20.. relating to our enquiry No. 921/KED and wish to place an order for the following items:

QTY.	DESCRIPTION	U. PRICE	T. PRICE
5,000	Rubberized spindles for Northrop looms	£0.80	£4,000.00
	Khedival mail line (agency)		£40.00
	Legalization and certification		£150.00
	TOTAL PRICE FOB		£4,190.00

(SAY FOUR THOUSAND ONE HUNDRED AND NINETY POUNDS STERLING ONLY)

purchase order
 Kauforder
place an order
 einen Auftrag
 erteilen
item Position
qty = quantity
 Menge
description
 Beschreibung
u. price = unit price
 Einheitspreis
t. price = total price
 Gesamtpreis
rubberized spindle
 gummierte Spindel
loom Webstuhl,
 Webmaschine
legalization
 Beglaubigung
certification
 Bescheinigung

39

TERMS

PRICES The above prices are firm and subject to no future change and are quoted FOB, packing included.

N.B. Kindly let us have a new Proforma Invoice in 10 (ten) copies, showing FOB prices, fixed delivery period and terms of payment.

PAYMENT Against a confirmed L/C only. Should any extension of the validity of the credit be necessary as a result of your being at fault, extra expenses incurred will be charged to you.

N.B. This order is subject to the approval of the appropriate Egyptian authorities and to the opening of the necessary credit in your favour.

DELIVERY 4 months from opening of L/C.

INSURANCE & FREIGHT As per our circulars enclosed.

CONDITIONS OF SHIPMENT Shipment by container is not allowed.
Shipment to be effected through:

KHEDIVAL MAIL LINE (AGENCY)
AIRWORK HOUSE
35 PICCADILLY
L O N D O N

We look forward to receiving your confirmation and remain

Yours faithfully
SOCIÉTÉ MISR DE FILATURE
ET DE TISSAGE FIN
...

firm fest
be subject to unterliegen
packing included einschließlich Verpackung
pro-forma invoice Pro-forma-Rechnung
fixed delivery period feste Lieferzeit
term of payment Zahlungsbedingung
confirmed L/C bestätigtes Akkreditiv
extension Verlängerung
validity Gültigkeit
be at fault im Verzug sein, auch: im Unrecht sein
extra expenses Zusatzkosten
incur auftreten
shipment Verschiffung
confirmation Bestätigung

Auftragsbestätigung
Confirmation of Order

➡ Briefe 18, 20 – 22

1 November 20..

Your ref.: 5769F/KED
Our ref.: GE/tt

Société Misr de Filature
et de Tissage Fin
KAFR EL DAWAR A.R.E.
EGYPT

Dear Sirs

Thank you for your letter of 17 October.

We hereby confirm your Purchase Order No. 5769
F/KED for 5,000 rubberized spindles for Northrop
looms, total price £4,190.00, FOB U.K. port, payment to be made by confirmed L/C.

We note your Conditions of Shipment and confirm
that the order will be effected as per the provisions
of your Insurance and Freight Circulars.

As requested we enclose a new pro-forma invoice
and ten copies thereof.

We trust the goods will arrive punctually and in
good condition and look forward to doing further
business with you in the future.

Yours faithfully
LUPTON BROS LTD

G. Etherington
Export Manager

Encs

rubberized spindle
 gummierte Spindel
loom   Webstuhl,
 Webmaschine
confirmed L/C
 bestätigtes Akkre-
 ditiv
note
 hier: feststellen, zur
 Kenntnis nehmen
effect   ausführen
as per   gemäß
provision
 Vorkehrung,
 Bestimmung
**Insurance and
 Freight Circular**
 Versicherungs- und
 Frachtrundbrief
trust
 glauben, vertrauen

➡ Briefe 18, 19, 21, 22

Société Misr de Filature
et de Tissage Fin
KAFR EL DAWAR A.R.E.
EGYPT

INSURANCE AND FREIGHT CIRCULAR

Dear Sirs

Further to our attached order we wish to draw your attention to our Insurance & Shipping Instructions and would point out that they are also those observed by ourselves.

1. SHIPPING METHOD
(a) Goods must be transported in the hold of the ship.
(b) Shipping to be effected using ships not more than 20 years old and also according to the Institute of London Underwriters classification clause.

2. SHIPPING INSTRUCTIONS
All cases should be marked S.M. followed by the number of the case, followed by the total number of cases in the consignment.

Example: If the cases are part of order 8706 and the total number of cases in the consignment amounts to 4, the cases should be marked:

S.M./8706/1/4   S.M./8706/2/4   S.M./8706/3/4
S.M./8706/4/4

When despatching the order please airmail us the NAME of the SHIP on which the goods are to be shipped and the number of the purchase order relating to the consignment. This information will be of great assistance to us in tracing the goods upon their arrival at port and in proceeding with their clearance through customs immediately, thus avoiding delay.

...../2

attached beigefügt
shipping method
  Art der Verschiffung
hold Laderaum
  (eines Schiffes)
cargo-bearing ship
  die Ladung beför-
  derndes Schiff
effect shipping
  Verschiffung durch-
  führen
according to
  entsprechend, gemäß
classification clause
  Klassifizierungs-,
  Bewertungsklausel
Underwriter
  Versicherer
consignment
  Sendung
despatch
  versenden
purchase order
  Kauforder
be of assistance
  hilfreich sein
trace *hier:* finden
proceed with
  hier: durchführen,
  erledigen
**clearance through
  customs**
  Zollabfertigung

3. DETAILS TO BE COMMUNICATED TO US

Please arrange for us to receive, at least 24 hours before sailing date, details of the consignment together with the following information to enable us to effect the required insurance:
(a) Name of the carrying ship
(b) Value of the goods despatched
(c) Port of loading

Before shipping any consignment, the value of which amounts to or exceeds E£30,000 (thirty thousand Egyptian pounds) at any one time, the above information must be communicated to us

TELEGRAPHICALLY

For ordinary orders the information, as specified above, can be sent by AIRMAIL letter.
N.B.   Failure to communicate details to us telegraphically, as specified above, will oblige us to hold you responsible for any decision prejudicial to ourselves in connection with our open insurance policy.

4. FREIGHT

"From port of despatch to Alexandria port", to be payable at destination, in "EGYPTIAN CURRENCY".

5. CLEARANCE

To enable us to clear the goods through customs please airmail us the appropriate invoice, packing and specification lists in 10 (ten) copies or more if possible.

In this respect we would draw your attention to the fact that by sending your invoices and packing lists etc. as requested you will save us a considerable amount of time and will, above all, avoid complications with our customs authorities.

Please follow the above instructions for all consignments sent against our orders. We depend on your co-operation for us to receive the information required in good time.

Yours faithfully
...

---

sailing date
  Abfahrtsdatum (bei Schiffen)
port of loading
  (Auf-)Ladehafen
amount to
  sich belaufen auf
exceed
  übersteigen
failure
  Unterlassung
oblige s.o.
  j-n zwingen, verpflichten
hold s.o. responsible
  j-n verantwortlich machen
prejudicial
  schädlich
open insurance policy Generalversicherungspolice
port of despatch
  Versandhafen
destination
  Bestimmungsort
currency Währung
clearance
  hier: Verzollung
invoice Rechnung
packing list
  Packliste
customs authorities
  Zollbehörden
depend on
  abhängen von
co-operation
  Mitarbeit
in good time
  rechtzeitig

21 Versandanzeige (Versandavis)
Advice of Despatch

➡ Briefe 18–20, 22

Lupton Bros Ltd
P.O. Box 8
Accrington
Lancashire BB5 1RJ
England

1 January 20..

Your ref.: 5769F/KED
Our ref.: GE/tt

Société Misr de Filature
et de Tissage Fin
KAFR EL DAWAR A.R.E.
EGYPT

Dear Sirs

Your Purchase Order No. 5769F/KED

We are pleased to inform you that the goods ordered as per the above mentioned purchase order have been despatched in accordance with your instructions.

They have been packed in 5 cases, 100 to a case. The cases are marked S.M./5769F/KED and numbered 1-5/5.

The consignment is being shipped on board m.v. "Egyptian Star", which is due to leave Southampton at the end of this month, arriving in Alexandria on 15 March.

We have handed our sight draft for £4,190.00 to the Arabian Bank, London together with the documents required under the terms of the L/C, namely: a complete set of clean, shipped on board Bs/L

.../2

purchase order
Kauforder
in accordance with
in Übereinstimmung mit
100 to a case
100 pro Kiste
on board a vessel
an Bord eines Schiffes
m.v. *Abkürzung für:*
motor vessel
Motorschiff
sight draft
Sichtwechsel
L/C *Abkürzung für:*
letter of credit
Akkreditiv
complete set
vollständiger Satz
clean B/L
reines Konnossement

endorsed to your order, marked in accordance with your specifications; one original and ten copies of the commercial invoice; a certificate of U.K. origin duly legalized by the Arab Republic of Egypt Representation; a declaration from the Egyptian Company for Maritime Transport "Martrans", evidencing that the goods have been shipped by them; a packing list; insurance certificate in triplicate.

The Arabian Bank has paid the sum.

We trust that the goods will be to your complete satisfaction and look forward to hearing from you again. We also enclose for your information some changes to our current price list.

Yours faithfully
LUPTON BROS LTD

G. Etherington
Export Manager

Enc

endorse
  indossieren
commercial invoice
  Handelsfaktura
certificate of origin
  Ursprungszeugnis
duly legalized
  vorschriftsmäßig
  beglaubigt
maritime transport
  Seetransport
evidence
  beweisen
packing list
  Packliste
insurance certificate
  Versicherungszertifikat
in triplicate
  in 3facher Ausfertigung
be to one's complete satisfaction
  zu j-s vollster Zufriedenheit ausfallen

22 Beschwerde - Reklamation
Complaint

➡ Briefe 18 – 21

20 March 20..

Lupton Bros Ltd
P.O. Box 8
ACCRINGTON
BB5 1RJ
England

Dear Sirs

Our Purchase Order No. 5769F/KED

With reference to the above-mentioned order for 5,000 rubberized spindles we regret to advise you that checks have revealed that the rubber at the base of approx. 40% of the spindles is in an unsatisfactory condition. It would appear that the rubber is perished owing to storage in strong sunlight or as a result of having been left outside for a prolonged period of time. We have airmailed you a sample spindle under separate cover for you to inspect yourselves.

You will appreciate that we are unable to install the defective parts in our looms and are therefore forced to run our mill at reduced capacity. This, in turn, has caused delays in delivery for our clients, who, should the delay continue, will have no alternative but to seek an alternative source of supply.

We therefore need 2,000 replacements in perfect condition immediately and would suggest that you despatch them to us by air freight, carriage paid.

We feel obliged to point out that your handling of this matter will determine whether we will be able to continue our business relationship in future.

Yours faithfully
SOCIÉTÉ MISR DE FILATURE
ET DE TISSAGE FIN
...

rubberized spindle gummierte Spindel
reveal (auf-)zeigen
to be perished spröde sein
storage Lagerung
in strong sunlight in starkem Sonnenlicht
prolonged verlängert
appreciate *hier:* verstehen
install einbauen
loom Webstuhl, Webmaschine
mill Fabrik
source of supply Lieferquelle
replacement Ersatz
by air freight per Luftfracht
carriage paid Fracht bezahlt
handling Behandlung

From: Krefeld.Maschinbau@telcom.de
To: purchase@landfill.com.uk
Date: 10 May 20..
Subject: Advice of Dispatch

Gentlemen:

As per your Order No. 231/ZH of April 30 we have despatched a VX 78 tire-shredder to you using InterTrans as freight forwarders. They, in turn, advise us that the machine will be shipped on board m.v. "Ariadne" which is due to leave Rotterdam on May 15 and will dock in Norfolk, Virginia at the end of June.

Under the FCA terms agreed the machine will be placed at your disposal at InterTrans's depot in St. Louis by June 30 at the latest.

Regards,
Günther Willmann
Export Manager

tire shredder
  Reifen-Shredder
freight forwarder
  Frachtspediteur
in turn   ihrerseits
m.v. = motor vessel
  Motorschiff
be due to leave
  fällig zur Abfahrt
  sein
dock   ins Dock
  gehen
depot   Depot,
  Lagerhaus

Stahlexport GmbH
Taunusstr. 12-14
46119 Oberhausen
Germany

2nd May 20..

Dear Mr Meier

Our Order 19345692 TI

Thank you for your telex of April 25 in which you state that the steel plates will be ready for dispatch and awaiting shipment in a fortnight's time.

In our L/C we stipulate that we require a commercial invoice, the B/L and the insurance certificate for shipment CIF Bangkok together with a quality control report. As regards this latter we have entrusted the company we name below with quality control and they will be contacting you in the next few days. They are:

SGS
Société Générale de Surveillance
German Office Hamburg

Would you please enclose this company's assessment with the documentation to be presented to both the issuing and the advising banks.

Thank you in advance for your help.

Yours sincerely
SOUTH EAST ASIA STEEL
...

steel plate Stahlplatte
await shipment zum Versand, zur Verschiffung bereitstehen
L/C = letter of credit Akkreditiv
commercial invoice Handelsfaktura
B/L = bill of lading Konnossement
insurance certificate Versicherungszertifikat
quality control report Qualitätskontrollbericht
entrust beauftragen, anvertrauen
assessment *hier:* Bericht
documentation Dokumentation, Papiere
issuing bank eröffnende Bank *(beim Akkreditiv)*
advising bank avisierende Bank *(beim Akkreditiv)*

10 April 20..

Diamantsägen Wilde GmbH
Ritterstraße 9
22089 Hamburg
GERMANY

Dear Mr Wilde

Our Enquiry PL/384 of 2nd March 19..
Your Offer No. 58391 of 21st March 19..

We are pleased to inform you that your DX 33 saw-blades wholly conform to our quality requirements. We should therefore like to place an order for 25 units, provided you can see your way clear to granting us a further rebate of 5% on your prices as quoted in the above-mentioned offer. We feel that the volume of the order we are interested in placing would justify this small concession.

However, to enable us to import these saw-blades into India we will need to apply for an import licence from our local Government authorities and would therefore ask you to send us a pro-forma invoice to include the following details:

- exact description of the goods
- unit and total price with discounts
- terms of payments and delivery CIF Calcutta
- packing list

We would be grateful if you would send the pro-forma invoice by registered mail. As soon as we have received the import licence, we shall telex our order to you and open the L/C with our bankers.

Yours sincerely
...

saw-blade	Sägeblatt
conform to	entsprechen
unit	Einheit, Stück
grant	gewähren
rebate	Nachlass
volume of the order	Auftragsvolumen
justify	rechtfertigen
import licence	Importlizenz
authority	Behörde
pro-forma invoice	Pro-forma-Rechnung
packing list	Packliste
by registered mail	per Einschreiben
open the L/C	das Akkreditiv eröffnen

Your ref: Fm/ly
Our ref: SM/52/ip

7 January 20..

Mr Arthur M Jones
Laser Engineering Ltd
1 Victoria Square
BIRMINGHAM
B1 1BD
United Kingdom

Dear Mr Jones

Your Order 835/XI of 15 Dec 19..

We are pleased to inform you that the articles, as per the above-mentioned order, were despatched by lorry yesterday. They will be shipped across the Channel on board SS Marina tomorrow and are due to arrive at your premises at the beginning of next week.

Please find enclosed our invoice No. 351 685 T for € 17,850.00 including all transport costs. We would ask you to settle it either by bank transfer or by cheque within 30 days, subject to the usual early payment discount of 3 per cent.

We trust that you will receive the goods in perfect condition and remain at your service for further deliveries at any time.

Yours sincerely
Daffur & Sattel GmbH

Hans Broich
Export Dept.

by lorry per Lkw
the Channel
  der Ärmelkanal
premises
  Geschäfts-, Büro-
  räume
transport costs
  Transportkosten
settle
  hier: bezahlen
by bank transfer
  per Banküberwei-
  sung
by cheque
  per Scheck
**the usual early pay-
ment discount**
  der für sofortige
  (baldige) Zahlung
  übliche Nachlass
further deliveries
  weitere Lieferun-
  gen

November 25, 20..

Seaboard Industries plc
Grand Avenue
HOVE
BN3 2LS
Great Britain

Ladies and Gentlemen:

As you know, we have been customers of your company for almost two years now and have always settled our invoices punctually by letter of credit in the pre-agreed way.

This is why we feel that we can now request you to grant us payment on open account terms for further deliveries, viz a 3-month payment period against presentation of your quarterly statement.

We feel that we have now earned this short-term credit facility, particularly because we aim to be placing further and possibly more substantial orders with you in the near future.

Awaiting your news with interest,

Sincerely yours,
Marting & Campals Inc.

Christopher P. Jefferson
Assistant Manager

settle an invoice
  eine Rechnung begleichen
letter of credit
  Akkreditiv
in the pre-agreed way in der vorher abgesprochenen Art und Weise
viz nämlich, das heißt
a 3-month payment period
  ein 3-monatiges Zahlungsziel
presentation
  Vorlage
quarterly statement
  vierteljährlicher Kontoauszug
short-term credit facility
  kurzfristige Kreditmöglichkeit
more substantial orders
  größere Aufträge

12 July 20..

Ms Maria de Lurdes Fontes Pereira
Fontes & Melo Ltda.
Rua de D. Afonso Henriques, 49
P-1300 Lisboa
PORTUGAL

Dear Ms Pereira

<u>Balancing of Our Quarterly Account
to June 30th 20..</u>

We confirm the receipt of your quarterly account showing a debit balance for us of £475.50.

After comparing your statement with our figures, however, we find that there is a discrepancy. According to our records our debit balance only amounts to £375.50. We have checked our invoices thoroughly and have been unable to find any irregularities in our payments. Could it be that your figure is a misprint?

We have of today advised our Invoicing Department to remit the equivalent of £375.50 in euros to your account by bank transfer and would request you to check your figures once again. Should you arrive at a figure differing from ours, please let us know, specifying the exact
nature of the difference of £100.00, for which we ourselves have no explanation.

We hope that this matter can be solved quickly and without any further inconvenience. For your information we are sending you enclosed a copy of our own statement.

Yours sincerely
...

quarterly	vierteljährlich
debit balance	Sollsaldo
statement	Kontoauszug
discrepancy	Unstimmigkeit
record	Eintragung
thoroughly	sorgfältig
irregularity	Unregelmäßigkeit, Unstimmigkeit
Invoicing Department	Rechnungsabteilung
remit	überweisen
equivalent	Gegenwert
arrive at a figure	auf eine Zahl kommen
differ	sich unterscheiden

The Clock Company Ltd
Addison Avenue
St. Albans
Herts SA3 1AD

25 September 20..

Patel Trading Co Ltd
Units 4-8 Industrial Estate
BLACKBURN
NL3 4WW

Dear Mr Patel

"Pocket Travelite" Alarm Clock

Our representative in the north of England informs us that you are in the market for electronic travelling alarm clocks. We are pleased to tell you that our latest model, the "Pocket Travelite", has just been launched and will most certainly suit your customers' requirements as regards price, quality, size and performance.

Our company has now been operating in this field for more than five years and in this time we have conducted in-depth market research into customer expectations. Our new "Pocket Travelite" has been tailor-made to correspond to the findings of our customer surveys and we have every confidence in its success. The new model's specifications are as follows:

Casing:	durable and shock-resistant matt plastic case in black, white or burgundy
Battery:	1.5 V, lasts one year on average
Size:	5 cm x 5cm x 3cm
Weight:	150 g

.../2

representative
Vertreter
be in the market for vertreiben, verkaufen wollen
launch
herausbringen, auf den Markt bringen
performance
Leistung
operate
hier: tätig sein
conduct führen
in-depth gründlich
market research
Marktforschung
tailor-made
maßgeschneidert
finding Ergebnis
survey
(Markt-)Studie
confidence Zuversicht, Vertrauen
durable haltbar
shock-resistant
stoßsicher

Features: illuminable digital display; snooze/re-peat function; alarm tone increases in volume

Guarantee: 12 months

Servicing: Free, except in cases of misuse, throughout guarantee period

Price: £12.00 per unit

Should you opt to place an initial order for over 100 units we will be pleased to grant you a discount of 10% on the price quoted.

We enclose a sample clock for your inspection to-gether with the full sales literature. Our conditions of sale and delivery are as is customary in the trade and are set out in detail in our brochure.

We look forward to your comments on our offer.

Yours sincerely
THE CLOCK COMPANY Ltd

A.P.T. Smith
Sales Manager

Encs

---

illuminable
 beleuchtbar
digital display
 Digitalanzeige
alarm tone
 Wecktonstärke
servicing
 Kundendienst
misuse Miss-
 brauch
guarantee period
 Garantiezeitraum
unit Einheit
opt
 sich entscheiden
initial order
 Erstauftrag
sample clock
 Probewecker
sales literature
 Werbematerial
customary üblich,
 gebräuchlich
comments
 Stellungnahme

9 April 20..

TEG GmbH
Castroper Hellweg 49
44805 Bochum
Germany

Attention: Herr Dix

Dear Mr Dix

Many thanks for your enquiry of March 20 in which you request us to quote prices, terms and delivery dates for our automatic mains-failure petrol-driven electricity generators.

Before submitting you an offer, however, we would be most grateful if you would provide us with a little more information as regards your exact requirements.

1. What voltage do you wish the generators to produce – 220-240 V or 380 V heavy-duty industrial power?

2. How many operating hours should the generators be able to run for before being refuelled?

3. Where will the generators be located? This is important as far as noise level and insulation are concerned. Our range includes both indoor and outdoor models.

We include our catalogue with this letter to give you an overview of our products and would be pleased to quote you on your exact requirements as soon as we have received the information requested.

Yours sincerely

...

mains-failure petrol-driven electricity generator mit Benzin angetriebenes Notstromaggregat
voltage Spannung
heavy-duty industrial power Hochleistungsindustriestrom, Starkstrom
operating hour Betriebsstunde
be refuelled wieder aufgetankt werden
be located angebracht werden
noise level Lärmpegel
insulation Isolierung
range Serie, Palette
overview Überblick

31 Annahme des Auftrags
Accepting an Order

Aw/wc
19 June 20..

Glas Strack
Ruhrallee 95–99
44139 Dortmund
GERMANY

Dear Sirs

Order No. LSG/50/93

We hereby confirm your order for laminated security glass as per your fax of 18 June.

We enclose our pro forma invoice as requested and would ask you to notify us as soon as the L/C has been opened. We will then be able to complete your order within a fortnight of receiving confirmation of the documentary credit from our bankers.

We look forward to hearing from you soon.

Yours faithfully
COOK'S GLASS AND GLAZING

Andrew Warmington
Export Manager

laminated security glass Schicht-sicherheitsglas
as per gemäß
pro forma invoice Pro-forma-Rechnung
notify benachrichtigen
L/C = letter of credit Akkreditiv
complete vervollständigen
within a fortnight innerhalb von 14 Tagen
confirmation Bestätigung
documentary credit Dokumentenakkreditiv

TD/TT
4 July 20..

INTRASHIP LTD
Eastern Dock
DOVER
DV9 6QY
England

Dear Mrs Horrocks

In the course of this week you will be receiving, FOB Dover, 2 containers of electric guitars and amplifiers marked S.W./93 1-2. They are to be shipped on the first available vessel to Rock Nouveau, 16 rue du Général Leclerc, Bayonne, France. Insurance will be covered by us.

Please make out the B/L to order in triplicate and send all three copies to ourselves. Please also notify us of the name of the vessel as soon as this is known to you.

Yours sincerely
MUSIC AND MORE LTD

Timothy Dearing
Sales Director

electric guitar
  elektrische Gitarre
amplifier
  Verstärker
available
  verfügbar
vessel Schiff
cover (ab-)decken
make out
  ausstellen
B/L = bill of lading
  Konnossement
to order an Order
in triplicate
  dreifach
notify
  benachrichtigen

33 Anfrage nach Frachtsätzen
Enquiry about freight rates

➡ Briefe 34, 35

PW/tt
10 November 20..

Specialised Shipping Services
Unit 20
Coppull Trading Estate
CHORLEY
PR7 5AY

Dear Sirs

Please quote us your most favourable freight rates
for the transport of 50 tonnes of palletised house
bricks, net weight 1 tonne per unit, for shipment
from Southampton to Tunis in the first two weeks
of December.

Please quote us assuming delivery F.O.B. Southampton stating details of shipping commission and
any further charges.

Yours faithfully
WHALEYS BRICKS LTD

Peter Whaley
Production Manager

quote anbieten
favourable günstig
freight rate
  Frachtsatz
palletise
  palettisieren, auf
  Paletten packen
brick Ziegelstein
unit Einheit, Stück
assume annehmen,
  voraussetzen
detail Einzelheit
commission
  Provision
further charges
  weitere Kosten

Frachtangebot
Freight Offer

34

➡ Briefe 33, 35

TT/si
15 November 20..

Whaleys Bricks Ltd
28 Mulberry Road
WINCHESTER
WI3 2WW

Dear Mr Whaley

Your Freight Enquiry of 10 November 20..

Thank you for your enquiry regarding the transport of 50 tonnes of palletised house bricks. Our offer is as follows:

> M.V. CLEETHORPES at £50 per metric tonne or 10 cubic metres, at steamer's option, with 4 lay days

As can be seen from the enclosed sailing card, the vessel is currently located in Marseille and is due to dock in Southampton on November 30th. Loading will commence as from December 1st with an additional charge of £250 for every day of demurrage.

If you accept this offer please forward us the charter party in quadruplicate to enable us to issue the necessary instructions to the ship's captain, Mr Terry Wrigglesworth.

We look forward to your early reply.

Yours sincerely

Theresa Templeton
Specialised Shipping Services

freight enquiry
 Frachtanfrage
at steamer's option
 nach Wahl des
 Dampfers *(gemeint
 ist hier die Ree-
 derei)*
lay day Liegetag
sailing card
 Schiffsfahrplan
currently zurzeit
dock
 ins Dock fahren
load (auf-)laden
commence
 beginnen
as from ab
additional charge
 zusätzliche Gebühr
demurrage
 Überliegezeit
forward schicken
charter party
 Charterpartie
in quadruplicate
 vierfach

35 Annahme des Frachtangebots
Acceptance of freight offer

➡ Briefe 33, 34

TW/tt
21 November 20..

Specialised Shipping Services
Unit 20
Coppull Trading Estate
CHORLEY
PR7 5AY

Fax: 00 44 1524 55057

Dear Ms Templeton

Thank you for your freight offer for palletised house bricks dated 15 November, which we are pleased to accept as follows:

> M.V. CLEETHORPES at £50 per metric tonne or 10 cubic metres, at steamer's option, with 4 lay days

The consignment of house bricks is from Redland Cement Ltd, Unit 10, Greenfields Industrial Estate, Reading and will be delivered F.O.B Southampton by Gotruck Haulage Ltd on December 1st.

You will be receiving the charter party in quadruplicate by separate post in the course of this week.

We hope that there will be no reason for delay of any sort and look forward to our order being shipped as agreed.

Yours sincerely
WHALEYS BRICKS LTD

Terry Whaley
Managing Director

---

palletised house bricks auf Paletten gepackte Hausziegel
consignment Sendung
Industrial Estate Industriegelände, Gewerbegebiet
by separate post mit getrennter Post
delay Verzögerung
of any sort irgendeiner Art

15 June 20..

Lion Assurance Ltd
42 Leadenhall St
LONDON
EC1 322

Dear Sirs

We have just taken delivery of a consignment of 200 bales of raw silk which was insured by yourselves. The merchandise was shipped on S.S. Anastasia, which docked in Plymouth on June 10. When our agents inspected the load they discovered that 15 of the bales were spoiled as a consequence of a storm in the South China Sea (survey report included).

We are therefore placing a claim for the damaged goods with you, the details of which are as follows:

Sea-damage 15 bales		
raw silk £1,000 per bale		£15,000.00
Additional expenses		£48.00
	Total	£15,048.00

Please arrange to have this sum transferred to our account with the Bergmann Bank in Düsseldorf.

We include all documentation related to this consignment as follows:

1. Insurance certificate
2. Survey report
3. Freight forwarder's invoice
4. Copy of the B/L
5. Ship broker's refusal to grant our claim

We trust you will be able to settle the matter swiftly.

Yours faithfully
...

---

consignment Sendung
bale Ballen
raw silk Rohseide
merchandise Ware
load Ladung
survey report Gutachterbericht
place a claim eine Forderung anmelden
sea-damage Seeschaden
arrange veranlassen
documentation Unterlagen
be related with zusammenhängen mit
insurance certificate Versicherungszertifikat
freight forwarder Frachtspediteur
B/L = bill of lading Konnossement
ship broker Schiffsmakler

37 Warenanalyse
Analysis of goods

➡ Brief 38

21 October 20..

Cornwall Plastics Ltd
49 Torrington Road
PENZANCE
PE3 9IK

Dear Sirs

4,200 KG POLYETHERESTER OF SILICIC ACID

We have duly examined the above mentioned con-signment and are pleased to submit our "Clean Report of Findings" to you as follows:

Goods submitted for inspection: 4,200 kg polyester of silicic acid as per pro-forma invoice No. 91900252 dated 1 October 20..

Seller: Cornwall Plastics Ltd
Penzance PE3 9IK,
Cornwall, UK

Importer: Slumberland Foam Inc.
92 Fence Rail Road
Pittsburgh
Pennsylvania PA49721
USA

FOB value: US$ 19,812.00
CFR value: US$ 20,412.00

Country of supply: Great Britain
Quantity: 20
Packing: drums

Gross weight: 4,543.00 kg
Net weight: 4,200.00 kg

Marks: CP/PSA92/1-20

...../2

silicic acid
  Kieselsäure
polyetherester
  Polyätherester
consignment
  Sendung
report of findings
  Untersuchungsbe-richt
submit
  vorlegen
pro-forma invoice
  Pro-forma-Rechnung
gross weight
  Bruttogewicht
net weight
  Nettogewicht
mark
  Markierung

FINDINGS

1. Quality: The quality of the goods submitted
to us for inspection has been found
to comply with the documents
presented to us inasmuch as their
examination is within our mandate.
2. Quantity: The quantity of goods is as stated
above under the rubric "Goods
submitted for inspection"
3. Price: Seller's final Invoice No. 0107689
dated 3 October 20.. showing a CFR
value of US$ 20412.00 has been sub-
mitted to us and we have compared
and found acceptable the FOB value
of US$ 19849.97 (say ONE NINE
EIGHT FOUR NINE POINT NINE
SEVEN U.S. DOLLARS)
4. Loading: Scheduled to be shipped at Plymouth
on board S.S. Morning Star as per
B/L No. D5 dated September 25th 20..

REMARKS

This document is valid only if signed by an
authorised representative of Trueworth Ltd and
accompanied by the following documents:
- negotiable bill of lading or equivalent evidence
of shipment to the USA
- copy of Seller's Final Invoice certified by Trueworth Ltd

This Clean Report of Findings in no way releases
the Sellers from their contractual obligations to the
Importers.

Yours faithfully
TRUEWORTH LTD - ASSESSORS
...

comply with   über-
einstimmen mit
inasmuch as
insoweit als
mandate
hier: Auftrag
rubric   Rubrik
final invoice   end-
gültige Rechnung
find acceptable
annehmbar, in Ord-
nung finden
scheduled   geplant
ship   verschiffen
B/L = bill of lading
Konnossement
authorised
ermächtigt, bevoll-
mächtigt
**negotiable bill of
lading**   begebbares
(negoziierbares)
Konnossement
equivalent
gleichwertig
certify   beglaubigen
release from
befreien von
**contractual obliga-
tion**   vertragliche
Verpflichtung
obligation to
Verpflichtung
gegenüber

38 Auftragsbestätigung des Spediteurs
Freight forwarder confirms order

➡ Brief 37

Intertrans Ltd
Units 2–10
Marine Walk
Plymouth
PL1 4RF

Our ref: 0123/34218Z
12 January 20..

Cornwall Plastics Ltd
49 Torrington Road
PENZANCE
PE3 9IK

Dear Sirs

We are pleased to confirm that your shipping and on-carriage instructions regarding the consignment mentioned below will be complied with as requested.

The documentation relating to the consignment will be forwarded to you in accordance with your wishes as stated in our previous correspondence.

Consignor:	Cornwall Plastics Ltd
	49 Torrington Road
	Penzance
	PE3 9IK
	Cornwall
Consignee:	Slumberland Foam Inc.
	92 Fence Rail Road
	Pittsburgh
	Pennsylvania PA49721
	USA
Consignment:	2,400 kg (20 drums) polyester of silicic acid

.../2

shipping instructions Verschiffungsanweisungen
on-carriage instructions Weiterbeförderungsanweisungen
consignment Sendung
comply with entsprechen, befolgen
relating to sich beziehend auf
forward senden, schicken
in accordance with in Übereinstimmung mit
consignor Übersender, Konsignant
consignee Empfänger, Konsignatar
silicic acid Kieselsäure

Marks:	CP/PSA92/1-20
Total weight:	4,543.00 kg
Shipped on:	10 January 20..
Vessel:	M.S. Morning Star
Destination:	Pittsburgh, Pennsylvania, USA

Should any delay arise or any change in procedure prove necessary, we will notify you as appropriate.

Assuring you of our best attention at all times

Yours faithfully
INTERTRANS LTD

Philip Jones
Manager

cc: Thomas Branscope
    Industrial Shipments Dept.

mark Markierung
vessel Schiff
M.S. = motorship
 Motorschiff
destination
 Bestimmungsort
delay Verzögerung
arise auftreten
procedure
 Vorgehen, Verfahrensweise
prove necessary
 sich als notwendig erweisen
notify
 benachrichtigen
as appropriate
 in geeigneter Weise

39 Auftragsbestätigung
Confirmation of order

From: jim.peters.ltd@te.com.uk
To: Band.A@sfv.de
Date: 10 August 20..
Subject: Order confirmation for Superlite
          Disk-Boxes of July 30

Gentlemen:

Your Order of July 30

Thank you for the above mentioned e-mail order for 500 3.5" Superlite Disk-Boxes as described in the August edition of Chip-Talk USA.

We have mailed the merchandise to you by surface mail and debited $960 to your account as stated. We expect the goods to arrive by the end of the month.

We look forward to the pleasure of doing further business with you in the near future.

Sincerely yours,

Marvin J. Wallis
Export Sales

as described
  wie beschrieben
edition
  Ausgabe
mail
  (per Post) schicken
surface mail
  (gewöhnliche) Postzustellung
debit
  belasten

Spediteur fordert Versanddokumente für Zollabfertigung an
Freight forwarder requests documents for custom clearance

40

➡ Briefe 41–47

EUROFREIGHT LTD
49 Tenterlowe Lane
Hillingdon
Middlesex MU8 8DE
e-mail: eurofreight@aol.com.uk

AG/MM
24 March 20..

Glaxo Chemicals Ltd
237 Sutton Common Road
LONDON
SW11 3BY

Dear Sirs

<u>Export Consignment to Budapest, Hungary</u>

We refer to the following shipping order:

Consignee:	Budapesti Vegyi Müvek Budapest XII Radnoti Miklos Utca 23 1367 Magyarorszag (Hungary)
Consignment:	10,565 kg bitumen (15 drums) (value £13,300)
Order No.:	191/1.93 (as per your fax of 12 March ..)
Delivery:	3–4 weeks after receipt of L/C
Hauliers:	Ungarocamion, Budapest

Your customer, Budapesti Vegyi Müvek, has requested us to collect the above consignment using Ungarocamion hauliers and forward it in accordance with his instructions to Hungary.

Please therefore let us have details of either the

...../2

shipping order
  hier: Verschiffungs-,
  Versandauftrag
haulier
  Lkw-Spediteur
**L/C = letter of
  credit** Akkreditiv
**documentary
  collection**
  Dokumenteninkasso
**B/E = bill of ex-
  change** Wechsel
**Bs/L = bills of lad-
  ing**
  Konnossemente

L/C or the documentary collection (B/E, Bs/L) agreed, to enable us to progress forwarding arrangements and issue a forwarder's receipt.

For customs clearance we require:

For Export

• Export notificaton or export declaration

For Import into Hungary

• Commercial Invoice in triplicate
• Packing specification in triplicate

Should you require any further details or information please do not hesitate to call us on 0181 580 4971 or fax us on 0181 580 4862, or send us an e-mail.

Yours faithfully
EUROFREIGHT LTD

Arnold Graham
Transport Controller

progress
   vorantreiben
forwarding arrangement
   Versandverein-
   barung
issue   ausstellen
forwarder's receipt
   Spediteurübernah-
   mebescheinigung
customs clearance
   Verzollung
export notification
   Exportbenachrichti-
   gung
hesitate   zögern

➡ Briefe 40,
42–47

Benson Bank Plc
6 Feather Lane
London
EC2 7HK

Our ref.: ATX 4977124
20 February 20..

Glaxo Chemicals Ltd
237 Sutton Common Road
LONDON
SW11 3BY

Dear Sirs

We confirm receipt of the documents listed below for collection. Collection will be in accordance with your instructions and subject to our General Terms of Trade.

Your ref.:	ZBD Mr Johnson 0078911
Our ref.:	ATX 4977124
Drawee:	Budapesti Vegyi Müvek
	Budapest XII
	Radnoti Miklos Utca 23
	1367
	Magyarorszag (Hungary)
Collecting Bank:	Hungarian National Bank
	Foreign Trade Section
	Szabadsag Ter 8
	1850 Budapest
	Hungary
Payment:	at sight
Amount:	£13,300 + our charges

.../2

collection Inkasso
in accordance with
 in Übereinstim-
 mung mit
subject to gemäß
drawee (Wechsel-)
 Bezogener
collecting bank
 Inkassobank
Foreign Trade Sec-
 tion Auslands-
 abteilung
payment at sight
 Zahlung auf Sicht
amount Betrag
charges Gebühren

Documents: Commercial Invoice 5/5
                Forwarder's receipt 1/1
                Certificate of origin 1/1
                Cert. of analysis 1/1
                Bill of exchange 1/1

This confirmation of receipt is also a copy of our
collection order. Please notify us immediately in the
event of discrepancies.

Yours faithfully
BENSON BANK PLC

Terence Hill
Foreign Trade Section

Encs

commercial invoice
Handelsfaktura
forwarder's receipt
Spediteurübernah-
mebescheinigung
certificate of origin
Ursprungszeugnis
**certificate of analy-
sis**   Analysezerti-
fikat
bill of exchange
Wechsel
discrepancy
Unstimmigkeit

➡ Briefe 40, 41,
43–47

1 March 20..

Hungarian National Bank
Foreign Trade Section
Szabadsag Ter 8
1850 Budapest
Hungary

Dear Sirs

We enclose the documents listed below for collection:

Commercial invoice	5/5
Forwarder's receipt	1/1
Certificate of origin	1/1
Certificate of analysis	1/1
Bill of exchange	1/1

The above-mentioned is in respect of a consignment of 15 drums of bitumen (value € 13,300) to be shipped on March 8, 20.. from London to Budapest. Delivery of the goods is to be taken by the drawee.

Please release the documents on payment of the draft and arrange to have the proceeds of the transaction by S.W.I.F.T. or by airmail to our Lombard Street branch quoting reference No. ATX 4977124.

Please confirm receipt by S.W.I.F.T. or on the enclosed form. In the event of non-payment please advise us by S.W.I.F.T. or, should this not be possible, by airmail.

This order is subject to the "Uniform Rules for Collections" (1978 revision) International Chamber of Commerce Publication No. 322.

Yours faithfully
BENSON BANK Plc
...

commercial invoice Handelsfaktura
forwarder's receipt Spediteurübernahmebescheinigung
certificate of origin Ursprungszeugnis
certificate of analysis Analysezertifikat
bill of exchange Wechsel
drawee Bezogener
draft *hier:* Wechsel
proceeds Erlös
S.W.I.F.T. Society for Worldwide Interbank Financial Telecommunication Bankencomputersystem für internationale Überweisungen
Uniform Rules for Collections Einheitliche Richtlinien für Inkassi
International Chamber of Commerce Internationale Handelskammer

43 Reklamation wegen eines Transportschadens
Complaint about damage to goods in transit

➡ Briefe 40–42, 44–47

FACSIMILE COVER SHEET	
BUDAPESTI VEGYI MŰVEK	
From: Georg Zold Goods Inwards	To: Mr Terence Stamp Export Sales Manager Glaxo Chemicals Ltd London SW11 3BY ENGLAND
Fax No.: 01 6689	Fax No.: 0181 990 6752
Our ref.: UNG/009.92	Your ref.:
Date: 20 April 20..	No. of pages to follow: 4

Facsimile Cover Sheet Telefax-Deckblatt

20 April 20..

Dear Mr Stamp

10,565 kg bitumen (15 drums)

We took delivery of the above-mentioned consignment yesterday (19 April) and regret to inform you that 3 of the drums are badly dented with some leakage having occurred. We enclose photographs of the damage for your information and our insurance agent's survey report.

We suspect that the damage was caused in transit and would be grateful if you would arrange for

...../2

above-mentioned oben genannt
be dented eingebeult sein
leakage Auslaufen
occur auftreten, passieren
survey report Gutachten, Bericht
suspect vermuten
in transit beim Transit

replacements to be sent to us – carriage and insurance paid – by the end of the month when the entire consignment is due to be collected and taken to Siberia by our CIS customer.

This is a new customer with whom we hope to develop a substantial volume of business in the future. For this reason we are very concerned that the agreed timetable should not be changed.

We trust this matter can be settled swiftly and expect the replacement drums to arrive in good time to be forwarded.

Yours sincerely
Budapesti Vegyi Müvek

Georg Zold
Goods Inwards

Encs

arrange for
sorgen für
replacement
Ersatz
carriage Fracht
insurance
Versicherung
be due fällig sein
CIS GUS
settle in Ordnung
bringen
in good time
rechtzeitig
to be forwarded
um versandt zu
werden

44 Verweisung einer Beschwerde an den Spediteur
Referral of customer complaint to freight forwarder

➡ Briefe 40–43, 45–47

Your ref.: UNG/009.92
Our ref.: TS/tt

21 April 20..

Budapesti Vegyi Müvek
Budapest XII
Radnoti Miklos Utca 23
1367
Hungary

Dear Mr Zold

<u>15 Drums of Bitumen (10,565 kg)</u>

Thank you for your fax dated 20 April in which you refer to damage and leakage in the case of 3 of the drums delivered.

We would point out, however, that according to the forwarder's receipt all 15 drums were accepted for delivery in good order and can therefore only conclude that the damage occurred in transit whilst the goods were in the custody of Eurofreight Ltd, the haulage company. We therefore suggest you contact Eurofreight Ltd, who, in the light of our previous dealings with this company, will undoubtedly settle the matter swiftly and amicably.

As soon as liability has been established we will supply appropriate replacements. Alternatively, we are willing to despatch replacements immediately, carriage forward. Should you wish us to do so please fax us to this effect.

Yours sincerely
GLAXO CHEMICALS LTD

Terence Stamp
Export Sales Manager

damage Schaden
leakage Auslaufen
forwarder's receipt Spediteurübernahmebescheinigung
in good order ordnungsgemäß, in gutem Zustand
be in the custody of im Gewahrsam sein von
haulage company (Lkw-)Transportfirma
in the light of angesichts
swiftly schnell
amicably freundschaftlich
liability Haftpflicht, Haftung
establish feststellen
carriage forward unfrei
to this effect in diesem Sinn, diesbezüglich

Beschwerde über Transportschaden
Complaint about damage in transit

➡ Briefe 40–44, 46, 47

Our ref.: UNG/009.92.1
28 April 20..

Eurofreight Ltd
49 Tenterlowe Lane
HILLINGDON
MU8 8DE
England

Dear Sirs

15 Drums of Bitumen (10,565 kg)

We took delivery of the above-mentioned consignment on 19 April and note that 3 drums are damaged with leakage. Our suppliers, Glaxo Ltd., waive
liability and claim that the goods were delivered to
yourselves in good condition, as evidenced by the
carrier's receipt. We therefore have no alternative
but to hold you responsible for the damage, which
obviously occurred in transit. We include a copy of
the insurance agent's report and photographs of
the drums for your information.

Glaxo are prepared to supply us with replacements
at short notice - carriage forward - in order to enable us to meet our commitments to our customer
here. We have instructed them to supply us with 3
more drums and will forward the invoice to yourselves for payment.

We trust this matter will be solved to our mutual
satisfaction.

Yours faithfully
BUDAPESTI VEGYI MÜVEK
...

consignment Sendung
waive liability Haftung ablehnen
in good condition in gutem Zustand
evidenced bewie-sen, nachgewiesen
carrier's receipt Übernahmebeschei-nigung des Fracht-führers
have no alternative but keine andere Möglichkeit haben als
hold s.o. respon-sible j-n verant-wortlich machen
insurance agent Versicherungsagent
at short notice kurzfristig
to meet one's com-mitments seinen Verpflichtungen nachkommen
to our mutual satis-faction zu unserer gegenseitigen Zu-friedenheit

46 Verweisung einer Beschwerde an den Versicherer
Referral of customer complaint to insurance company

➡ Briefe 40–45, 47

Your ref.: UNG/009.92.1
5 May 20..

Budapesti Vegyi Müvek
Budapest XII
Radnoti Miklos Utca 23
1367
HUNGARY

Dear Mr Zold

Thank your for your letter of 28 April in which you give details of damage to 3 drums of bitumen delivered by ourselves to your company on April 19th. We regret the inconvenience caused and feel you acted correctly by having the damage assessed by your insurance agent.

We have looked into the matter and examined the driver's log for the trip in question and have discovered that our vehicle was involved in a minor accident. The case is currently in the hands of our lawyers and should be settled by the end of the month. Our insurance cover provides for indemnification for any eventuality so we would therefore request you to approach our insurers, whose name and address are as follows:

Accident Insurance Europe
Insurance House
London EC1A 4WW
England.

Please quote policy No. GLX/342-00/93.

We trust the matter will be settled to your satisfaction in due course.

Yours sincerely
EUROFREIGHT LTD
...

inconvenience Unannehmlichkeit
act correctly richtig handeln
have the damage assessed den Schaden feststellen lassen
look into the matter die Sache untersuchen
log *hier:* Fahrtenbuch
vehicle Fahrzeug
be involved verwickelt sein
lawyer Rechtsanwalt
insurance cover Versicherungsdeckung
indemnification Entschädigung
eventuality Möglichkeit
approach *hier:* sich wenden an
policy Police

➡ Briefe 40–46

Budapesti Vegyi Müvek
Budapest XII
Radnoti Miklos Utca 23
1367
Hungary

Policy No.: GLX/342-00/93.
14 May 20..

Insurance Accident Europe
Insurance House
LONDON
EC1A 4WW
England

Dear Sirs

<u>15 Drums of Bitumen (10,565 kg)</u>

We took delivery of the above-mentioned consignment on 19 April and regret to inform you that 3 of the drums are badly dented with some leakage having occurred. We enclose photographs of the damage for your information and our insurance agent's survey report.

We have so far approached both Glaxo Chemicals Ltd, the suppliers, and Eurofreight Ltd, the haulage company, and as neither of these parties will accept liability we are turning to you on the advice of Eurofreight Ltd to claim compensation.

Please refer to the enclosed insurance agent's survey report for details of the damage and an assessment of the replacement costs. We also enclose copies of all documentation authenticated by the British Consulate in Budapest.

We trust you will send us the necessary claims forms at your earliest convenience to ensure that this matter is settled once and for all.

.../2

insurance agent
Versicherungsagent
survey report
Schadensbericht, Gutachten
supplier Lieferant
accept liability
Haftung übernehmen
on the advice of
auf Anraten von
claim compensation
Schadenersatz fordern
replacement
Ersetzung, Ersatz
documentation
Dokumente, Unterlagen
authenticate
beglaubigen, beurkunden
claim form
(Schadens-)Forderungsformular
ensure sicherstellen
once and for all
ein für alle Mal

We have already incurred losses because of this situation and reserve the right to make a claim for them.

We also wish to point out that, should we incur further losses as a result of our customer's cancelling the order owing to delay in delivery, we will also claim compensation for loss of business.

We look forward to your early reply in this matter.

Yours faithfully
BUDAPESTI VEGYI MÜVEK

Georg Zold
Goods Inwards

Encs

incur further losses
weitere Schäden erleiden
cancel the order
den Auftrag stornieren
delay in delivery
Lieferverzug
loss of business
entgangenes Geschäft

Bitte um Übersendung einer Pro-forma-Rechnung
Request for pro-forma invoice

From: Hamacher.Maschinenbau@te.com.de
To: JMJ.engineering@network.uk
Date: 15 May 20..
Subject: Our order no. 342/93 for piston rings

Dear Mr. Marshall

In order to obtain an import licence for the items ordered and to open the L/C, we require a pro-forma invoice containing price estimates and quantities.

We would be obliged if you would send us this by the end of the month to enable us to effect delivery as soon as possible.

Our postal address is:
Hamacher Maschinenbau GmbH
Zeissweg 39
D-87700 Memmingen

Yours sincerely
HAMACHER MASCHINENBAU GMBH

Walter Schlimm
Purchasing Manager

piston ring
  Kolbenring
import licence
  Importlizenz
item Posten,
  Position
**L/C = letter of
  credit** Akkreditiv
contain enthalten
estimate Schätzung
effect delivery
  Lieferung ausführen
Purchasing Manager
  Einkaufsleiter

AM/GH
27 April 20..

New Form Plastics Moulds Ltd
Unit 19
Needham Industrial Estate
OXFORD
OX8 7HH
England

Dear Sirs

As the value of the plastics moulds ordered by ourselves in our letter of February 28 exceeds £50,000 sterling, we require a customs invoice for the customs authorities here to enable them to assess import duty. We would therefore be most grateful if you would issue this document at your earliest convenience to enable us to complete the necessary formalities at this end.

Yours faithfully
MUTUMBUKO PLASTICS LTD

Arnold Twumasi
Import Manager

plastic mould
  Plastik-Form(stück)
exceed   übersteigen
customs invoice
  Zollrechnung
customs authority
  Zollbehörde
to assess   feststellen
import duty
  Einfuhrzoll
**at your earliest
  convenience**
  so schnell wie
  möglich
formality
  Formalität
at this end
  hier, bei uns

Bitte an Lieferanten um Gewährung eines offenen Zahlungsziels
Requesting open account payment terms with a supplier

50

➜ Brief 51

JT/GG
29 March 20..

C. & W. Berry Industrial Paints
Wellford Mill Lane
Leyland
PRESTON
PR5 1LE

Dear Mr Berry

Further to our recent telephone call regarding the supply of industrial paints for our retail outlets throughout the UK, I am pleased to advise you that we are prepared to stock your products for a trial period of 90 days as from the beginning of April.

We feel, for the time being, that open account terms with regular quarterly statements would be most appropriate.

Please invoice us here at Head Office in Manchester for all deliveries to all outlets itemising the goods supplied to show unit and total prices and indicating which of our branches have been supplied.

We trust this arrangement will prove satisfactory and would be pleased to receive written confirmation by mail or fax by return.

Yours sincerely
THE CROWN TRADE CENTRE

John Tidmarsh
Head Buyer

industrial paint
  Industriefarbe
retail outlet
  Einzelhandelver-
  kaufsstelle
stock lagern
trial period
  Versuchszeitraum
open account terms
  offenes Zahlungsziel
quarterly statement
  vierteljährlicher
  Kontoauszug
invoice berechnen,
  in Rechnung stellen
Head Office
  Hauptgeschäfts-
  stelle
itemise (einzeln)
  aufführen, spezifi-
  zieren
unit price
  Einheitspreis
total price
  Gesamtpreis
Head Buyer
  Chefeinkäufer

51 Kontenausgleich (Übersendung Kontoauszug)
Settlement of account (sending a statement)

➡ Brief 50

WB/JS
2 July 20..

THE CROWN TRADE CENTRE
23–41 Gresham Road
MANCHESTER
MA4 1HQ

Dear Mr Tidmarsh

Please find enclosed our statement of account for the period April 1st – June 30th.

As requested we have itemised all deliveries to include unit and total prices and have indicated which of your stores was supplied in each case.

We have deducted £47.92 from the price of the consignment of "Dawn Beige Coverplus Vinyl" delivered to your Preston branch on June 23rd owing to the poor shade match with the previous batch. We trust this will prove acceptable to you.

Please pay by transfer to our account with the Newtown Bank in Manchester (Account No. 2346731).

We look forward to doing further business with you and remain

Yours sincerely
C. & W. BERRY INDUSTRIAL PAINTS

William Berry
Co-director

Enc

statement of account Kontoauszug
deduct abziehen
consignment Sendung
branch Filiale
owing to wegen
shade Farbton
match *hier:* Übereinstimmung
batch Posten, Partie
acceptable annehmbar
pay by transfer durch Überweisung zahlen

Zahlung durch Banküberweisung (SWIFT)
Payment by bank transfer (SWIFT)

IG/PO
26 June 20..

Benson Bank plc
34–38 Market Place
NEW MALDEN
KT3 5TZ

Dear Sir

<u>Our Account No. 789315</u>

Please transfer the sum of

£5,423.00

to the account of Esser & Co., Wirtschaftswerbung GmbH in Witten, Germany in respect of their invoice No. 92/4/AUSL./4093.

The account details are as follows:
Account holder: Esser & Co.
Account No.:   789046001
Branch Code: 45240056

We would be grateful if you would arrange for payment to be effected by SWIFT to ensure that the funds arrive by the end of the month.

Yours faithfully
VANTAGE ADVERTISING

Iain Gowe
European Campaigns Manager

transfer
  überweisen
account   Konto
in respect of
  bezüglich
detail   Einzelheit
account holder
  Kontoinhaber
branch code
  Filialcode, Bank-
  leitzahl
arrange for
  veranlassen
effect   durchführen
ensure
  sicherstellen
funds   (Geld-)
  Mittel

53 Erste Mahnung
First reminder

➡ Briefe 54–57

AL/GL
12 July 20..

Satic Optik GmbH
Kemnaderstr. 33
58456 Witten
Germany

Attention: Herr Holler

Dear Herr Holler

May we draw your attention to the enclosed brochure containing details of our new multifocal, light-sensitive lenses, which are especially suited for those frequently engaged in outdoor pursuits. We feel that we have "beaten the others past the post" as far as marketing this new, low-price product from the USA is concerned and are sure that it will find a ready market in Germany, the home of high-class optics.

May we also draw your attention to our invoice No. 1892Z/5/93 dated May 1st which, according to our records, is so far unpaid. We feel sure that this is due to an oversight on your part and would appreciate payment within the next few days. If payment has already been effected please disregard this letter.

We look forward to hearing from you soon.

Yours sincerely
NORTHERN OPTICS LTD

Alan Gore
Credit Controller

Enc

brochure Broschüre, Prospekt
contain details Einzelheiten enthalten
multifocal lense Mehrstärkenglas
light-sensitive lichtempfindlich
outdoor draußen, im Freien
pursuit Beschäftigung, Tätigkeit
to beat the others past the post die anderen aus dem Rennen werfen
low-price preisgünstig
find a ready market einen guten Absatz finden
optics Optikartikel

Zweite Mahnung
Second reminder

AL/GL
10 August 20..

Satic Optik GmbH
Kemnaderstr. 33
58456 Witten
Germany

➡ Briefe 53,
55 – 57

Attention: Herr Holler

Dear Herr Holler

Your Ref.:	023/499
Account No.:	SO/894377
Balance Due:	€ 4,231.92
Due Date:	15 June 20..

I am disappointed to note that, despite our previous reminder of 12 July, your account with us still remains unpaid. You will recall from our Conditions of Sale that all outstanding balances due to us must be paid within thirty days after receipt of our invoice. By placing an order with us you indicated your agreement to our terms. According to my records no query has been raised with regard to the goods delivered or the accounts rendered.

Under the circumstances I would be grateful if you could arrange for the above sum to be paid by return. Should you fail to do so I shall have no alternative but to add interest to the balance at the rate of 25% per annum as prescribed by our Conditions of Sale.

Yours sincerely
NORTHERN OPTICS LTD

Alan Gore
Credit Controller

balance due
Sollsaldo
due date
fälliges Datum
conditions of sale
Verkaufsbedingungen
outstanding balances ausstehende Salden
within 30 days
innerhalb von 30 Tagen
receipt Erhalt
with regard to the accounts rendered
bezüglich der vorgelegten Rechnungen
by return
umgehend
interest Zinsen
at the rate of 25% per annum
zu einem Satz von 25% im Jahr
as prescribed
wie vorgeschrieben

55 Letzte Mahnung
Final demand

➡ Briefe 53, 54, 56, 57

AL/GL
18 August 20..

Satic Optik GmbH
Kemnaderstr. 33
58456 Witten
Germany

Attention: Herr Holler

Dear Mr Holler

Balance Due: € 4,231.92
Interest Accrued: € 352.58

Despite repeated reminders your account still remains unpaid. Unless I receive a remittance covering all balances due within four days from the date of this letter I will have no alternative but to instruct our solicitors to take legal action against you.

In this case proceedings will be instigated without further notice to regain the sum owed, the interest accrued for the outstanding period and the costs of legal action.

Yours sincerely
NORTHERN OPTICS LTD

Alan Gore
Credit Controller

interest accrued aufgelaufene Zinsen
remittance Überweisung
instruct anweisen
solicitor Anwalt
take legal action against you gerichtliche Schritte gegen Sie unternehmen
proceedings (gerichtliches) Verfahren
instigate *hier:* einleiten
without further notice ohne weitere Benachrichtigung
regain zurückerstattet bekommen
costs of legal action Kosten des gerichtlichen Verfahrens

FACSIMILE COVER SHEET	
Satic Optik D-58943 Witten	
From: Herr Holler Sales Manager	To: Alan Gore Credit Controller
Fax No.: +2302 276398	Fax No.: +1772 20936
Our ref.: 023/499	Your ref.: 1892Z/5/93
Date: 2 September 20..	No. of pages to follow: 1

➡ Briefe
53–55, 57

**Facsimile Cover
Sheet**
Telefax-Deckblatt

2 Sept 20..

Dear Mr Gore

Account No. SO/894377
Outstanding Balance

Please forgive us for not replying to your letters
earlier. We have recently undergone a major
restructuring of the company entailing a move to
more suitable premises on the outskirts of Witten
and a significant rationalisation of staffing levels.
This, in turn, has led to a number of problems in
the Accounts Department, which has now been
entirely re-organised. We are currently dealing with
a considerable backlog of administrative matters
and have, at the same time, been doing our best

.../2

undergo
durchmachen
restructuring
Neuordnung
entail
nach sich ziehen
premises
Geschäftsräume
outskirts Randge-
biet, Peripherie
staffing levels
Personalbestand
**Accounts Depart-
ment** Rechnungs-
abteilung
backlog Rück-
stand, Überhang

to keep up with the unexpectedly large influx of advance orders for our new light-sensitive lenses.

We would, under the circumstances, be grateful if you would permit us to prolong the draft until September 30, by which date we will have remitted all monies owing to you including interest accrued.

We trust you will agree to this proposal. You can rest assured that the matter will be settled by the end of the month.

Yours sincerely

Theodor Holler
Sales Manager

P.S.
Please note the address of our new premises:
Industriestr. 20–28, D-58943 Witten

influx
  Zufuhr, Zustrom
light-sensitive
  lichtempfindlich
draft   Tratte, *im Engl. auch häufig:* (akzeptierter) Wechsel
interest accrued
  aufgelaufene Zinsen
proposal
  Vorschlag

Gläubiger bereit, Teilzahlung zu akzeptieren
Creditor prepared to accept part-payment

➡ Briefe 53–56

AL/GL
3 September 20..

Satic Optik GmbH
Industriestr. 20–28
58943 Witten
Germany

Attention: Herr Holler

Dear Herr Holler

Your Account No.:   SO/894377
Total outstanding: € 4,584.40

We have received your fax of 2 September.

We find your proposal unacceptable, above all because of the inordinately long period of time that has elapsed since the first of our three reminders (12 July) and your response. This has led us to conclude that you are not interested in maintaining a business relationship with us in the long term.

We are, however, prepared to accept an immediate payment of € 2,500 accompanied by a draft drawn on yourselves at 30 d/s for € 2,162.75 in respect of the unpaid balance including interest accrued by expiry on October 4th. We enclose our new draft for your acceptance.

Please indicate by return whether you accept these terms or not. Should they prove unacceptable we will immediately initiate proceedings for the recovery of all monies due.

Yours sincerely
NORTHERN OPTICS LTD
...

Encl.

---

total outstanding
  gesamter ausstehender Betrag
inordinately
  übermäßig
period of time
  Zeitspanne
elapsed verstrichen
maintain
  aufrechterhalten
in the long term
  langfristig
accompanied by
  begleitet von
drawn on
  bezogen auf
30 d/s = days/sight
  30 Tage Sicht
expiry Fälligkeit
acceptance
  hier: Akzept
initiate proceedings
  (gerichtliche)
  Schritte einleiten
recovery
  hier: Eintreibung

58 Kunde entschuldigt sich für Zahlungsverzögerung
Customer apologises for delay in payment

June 17, 20..

Hudson Mechanical Engineering Inc.
782 Fairweather Street
Boston, MA 02116
USA

Ladies and Gentlemen:

We received your letter of 10 June and are sorry that there has been a delay in paying your Invoice No. 094/5/93.

We have unfortunately been hit by the economic downswing in Europe as a whole and in the engineering sector in particular, which has resulted in temporary financial difficulties for our company.

A considerable number of our customers have had to file applications for bankruptcy and, pending decisions in these cases, which could go on for months, we are not in a position to press them for payment. We have, nevertheless, been given assurances by our bankers that part-payment of your invoice is possible. We have therefore transferred 50% of the sum outstanding to your account.

With respect to the outstanding balance we are unfortunately compelled to request you to grant us an extension of a further 30 days for this sum. If you can see your way clear to granting us this facility please send us a draft at 30 d/s drawn upon ourselves to this effect, which we will accept and return to you immediately.

We trust you will understand our predicament, which, as you can see, is entirely due to circumstances beyond our control.

Sincerely yours,

...

economic downswing
wirtschaftlicher Rückgang
engineering sector
Technikbereich
file an application for bankruptcy
einen Konkursantrag stellen
press s.o. for payment   j-n auf Zahlung drängen
outstanding balance
ausstehender Saldo
draft at 30 d/s (days/sight)
30-Tage-Sichtwechsel
drawn upon ourselves
auf uns gezogen
predicament
(missliche) Lage
be due to circumstances beyond our control
auf Umstände außerhalb unserer Kontrolle zurückzuführen sein

28 February 20..

South Western Bank plc
Leadenhall Street
LONDON
EC1 4WW
England

Dear Sirs

Request for Assistance with Engaging a UK Agent

We are a major German supplier of fitted kitchen equipment with an annual turnover in the Federal Republic well in excess of €15m. We have so far been represented in the UK by Messrs Crowther & Tidmarsh, a firm of kitchen suppliers which has now ceased trading owing to the death of Mr Tidmarsh. It is for this reason that we are turning to you to ask for assistance in finding a suitable agent for our products.

The firm or individual in question would sell on our behalf on a commission basis, preferably through an already existing network of retail outlets throughout the UK and possibly Northern Ireland. We feel that a well-capitalised company would be able to stock a sufficient quantity of our products to give an impression of our wide range.

We would therefore be extremely grateful if you could recommend a suitable company. We would, of course, also be pleased if your bank would handle all payments arising from the business an agency network would generate.

We very much hope that you will be able to assist us in this matter and remain

Yours faithfully
KÜCHENSTUDIO MAUERMANN
...

fitted kitchen
  Einbauküche
annual turnover
  Jahresumsatz
cease trading
  aufhören Handel
  zu treiben
on our behalf
  für uns
commission basis
  Provisionsbasis
network
  Netz(werk)
retail outlet
  Einzelhandelsver-
  kaufsstelle
a well-capitalised
  company
  eine mit Kapital
  gut ausgestattete
  Gesellschaft
to stock
  auf Lager nehmen
range
  Produktserie
generate *hier:*
  mit sich bringen

60 Bewerbung um die Vertretung einer Firma
Application to become an agent for a firm

➡ Briefe 61, 62, 63

Modern Sports Sportkleidung
Bahnhofstr. 112
40489 Düsseldorf
Germany
E-mail: modern.sports@gmx.de

20 March 20..

Land & Hunter Sportswear Specialists
12 Thames Street
KINGSTON
KT1 1PF
England

Dear Sirs

Enquiry about Agency Agreement

In their latest information bulletin our bankers, the Gunzelmann Bank in Düsseldorf, publicised your request to them for assistance in finding an agent for your sportswear in Germany.

We have a comprehensive network of specialised retail sportswear outlets throughout North Rhine-Westphalia and, in addition, have branches in all major German cities. We understand from our bankers that you specialise in durable, waxed cotton clothing, lightweight boots, tents and survival gear. We feel there is excellent potential for such equipment here and, provided the quality is in keeping with our customers' expectations, would welcome an opportunity to market your products in the Federal Republic.

We would appreciate it, if you would send us comprehensive sales literature on your products together with a sample tent, waxed cotton anorak and perhaps any other items you feel will show off your goods effectively.

.../2

agency agreement
  Vertretervertrag
publicise
  bekannt machen
sportswear
  Sportkleidung
comprehensive
  groß, umfassend
retail outlet
  Einzelhandelsver-
  kaufsstelle
branch Filiale
durable haltbar
lightweight boots
  leichte Stiefel
tent Zelt
survival gear
  Überlebensaus-
  rüstung
potential
  Möglichkeit(en)
**welcome an oppor-
  tunity**
  eine Gelegenheit
  begrüßen

Should you require references, the Gunzelmann Bank in Düsseldorf will be pleased to supply you with any information you may desire.

We feel sure that this could well be the beginning of a successful business venture and look forward to hearing from you in the near future. For your information we enclose a brochure and further details of our organisation.

Yours faithfully
MODERN SPORTS SPORTKLEIDUNG

Theo Kohl
Managing Director

Enc

sales literature
Verkaufsmaterial
sample tent
Musterzelt
show off effectively
wirkungsvoll zur
Geltung bringen
**successful business
venture**
erfolgreiches
Geschäftsunter-
nehmen

61 Angebot einer Exklusivvertretung
Offer of sole agency

➡ Briefe 60, 62, 63

30 March 20..

Modern Sports Sportkleidung
Trautmann & Sander
Bahnhofstr. 112
40489 Düsseldorf
Germany

Dear Mr Kohl

Sole Agency Agreement

Many thanks for your letter of 20 March, in which you express an interest in marketing our goods.

We are, indeed, looking for an agent for our products in Germany and it sounds as if your organisation could well fit the bill. Our products are tremendously successful over here in the UK. Waxed cotton clothing is now all the rage and the market is expanding fast. We enclose the samples you request together with illustrated sales literature and our latest trade price-list. We feel sure that the quality will give you no grounds for complaint, as our products are truly state-of-the-art and used by top mountaineers throughout the world.

The Gunzelmann Bank describes your organisation as sound and efficient and therefore, provided you are satisfied with the samples, all that remains is for our lawyers to draft a sole agency agreement ready for signature.

We suggest a meeting here in Kingston to sign the agreement and to get to know each other a little better.

Yours sincerely
LAND & HUNTER
...

sole agency agreement Vertrag für eine Allein(Exklusiv-)vertretung
fit the bill ins Konzept passen
tremendously successful ungeheuer erfolgreich
be all the rage die große Mode sein
illustrated sales literature illustriertes Werbematerial
trade price-list Preisliste für den (Fach-)Handel
give no grounds for complaint keinen Grund zur Klage geben
state-of-the-art neuester Stand (der Technik)
sound *hier:* gesund
to draft an agreement einen Vertrag aufsetzen

➡ Briefe 60, 61, 63

Modern Sports Sportkleidung
Bahnhofstr. 112
40489 Düsseldorf
Germany
E-mail: modern.sports@gmx.de

15 May 20..

Land & Hunter Sportswear Specialists
12 Thames Street
KINGSTON
KT1 1PF
England

Dear Mr Land

Confirmation of Agency

After our very instructive and positive meeting in Kingston we should like to state once again the main points upon which we reached agreement as regards our future co-operation:

1. We are to act as your sole agents in Germany for the agreed period.

2. The conditions stated in the agreement are valid for a period of two years after the date of the agreement.

3. We undertake to trade with no imported products of a similar nature which could compete with the products to which this agreement relates.

4. Account sales will be submitted quarterly and we will accept your drafts on us for the net amount accruing from sales of your products.

5. We undertake to display a representative cross-section of your products in all of our retail outlets

...../2

instructive
aufschlussreich
sole agent
Allein(Exklusiv-)
vertreter
undertake
sich verpflichten
product of a similar
nature Produkt
ähnlicher Art
compete
konkurrieren
account sales
hier: Verkaufs-
abrechnung
submit vorlegen
quarterly
vierteljährlich
draft
Tratte, Wechsel
on us
auf uns gezogen
accrue entstehen

in Germany in such a manner as to bring them to the attention of a maximum number of customers.

We trust that you will send us written confirmation of these points in due course and look forward to receiving your draft of the agency agreement.

The final version will need to be translated into German, but that is something which we can organise here in Dusseldorf.

Yours sincerely
MODERN SPORTS SPORTKLEIDUNG

Theo Kohl
Managing Director

cross-section
Querschnitt
retail outlet
Einzelhandels-
verkaufsstelle
in due course
zu gegebener Zeit
agency agreement
Vertretervertrag

➡ Briefe 60, 61, 62

Modern Sports Sportkleidung
Bahnhofstr. 112
40489 Düsseldorf
Germany
E-mail: modern.sports@gmx.de

1 November 20..

Land & Hunter Sportswear Specialists
12 Thames Street
KINGSTON
KT1 1PF
England

Dear Mr Land

Report on First Quarter Sales

We are pleased to inform you that sales activity has been brisk throughout this first quarter with a balance of € 17,000 in your favour. On presentation of your draft drawn on us for this amount of 30 d/s it will be accepted and returned to you immediately, as agreed.

We feel that our advertising campaign, launched as it was at the end of the summer season, was particularly effective because waxed cotton jackets are most suited to weather conditions at this time of year. The new German TV series bought from Thames Televison entitled "Outdoor Style" featuring prominent British TV personalities wearing your company's anoraks has also certainly had a beneficial effect on sales. We enclose some material from the advertising campaign and press coverage of the TV series for your information.

.../2

first quarter sales Umsatz im ersten Quartal
brisk lebhaft
balance in your favour Saldo zu Ihren Gunsten
on presentation bei Vorlage
draft Tratte, Wechsel
advertising campaign Werbekampagne
waxed cotton gewachste Baumwolle
feature zeigen
beneficial nützlich, vorteilhaft
sales Umsatz, Verkäufe
turnover Umsatz

For the next quarter we expect an even greater turnover, particularly in the bigger men's sizes with large waist measurements. Please make sure that these sizes are available in greater numbers to accommodate the market here.

As regards pricing policy, we feel that the current weakness of the pound should be passed on to our customers and suggest an across-the-board price reduction of 10% on the trade prices quoted.

We look forward to your comments on this matter and are confident that the market will continue to offer considerable potential for the foreseeable future.

Yours sincerely
MODERN SPORTS SPORTKLEIDUNG

Theo Kohl
Managing Director

Encs

waist measurement
  Taillemaß
accommodate
  entgegenkommen
pricing policy
  Preispolitik
across-the-board
  global
trade price Preis
  an den (Fachhandel)
potential
  Möglichkeit(en)
foreseeable future
  absehbare Zukunft

Erkundigung über Versicherungssätze
Enquiry about insurance rates

➡ Briefe 65, 66

5 April 20..

Sovereign Assurance Ltd
London Regional Marine Branch
24 Lime Street
LONDON
EC3 7JE

Dear Sir or Madam

Please let us have your quotation for insurance cover against all risks, warehouse to warehouse, for a consignment of:

50 bales of raw silk from Liverpool to Marseille on board the vessel "M.S. Northern Star" of the M&P Line.

Replacement value is £5,000.

Cover is required as from June 1st.

Yours faithfully
Turnpike Trading Co. Ltd.

Ronald Soames
Director

quotation
 (Preis-)Angebot
insurance cover
 Versicherungs-
 deckung
warehouse
 Lager
consignment
 Sendung
bale Ballen
raw silk
 Rohseide
replacement value
 Ersatzwert
as from
 ab *(zeitlich)*

65 Versicherungsangebot
Insurance quotation

➡ Briefe 64, 66

10 April 20..

Turnpike Trading Co. Ltd.
Unit 5
Watery Lane Trading State
GUNNERBURY
MI5 3TH

Dear Sirs

Thank you for your letter of 5 April, in which you
ask for our quotation for:

Risk:	50 bales of raw silk, Liverpool – Marseille
Vessel:	M.S. Northern Star
Shipping company:	M&P Line
Value:	£5,000
Cover:	all risks, warehouse to warehouse
Dates:	as from 1 June 20..

We are please to quote you as follows:

15p%

This offer is subject to the silk being seaworthily
packed.

We look forward to your reply to this quotation
and remain

Yours faithfully
SOVEREIGN ASSURANCE LTD
...

risk Risiko
bale Ballen
raw silk
  Rohseide
vessel Schiff
shipping company
  Reederei
value Wert
cover
  Deckung
be subject to
  unterliegen
be seaworthily
  packed
  seemäßig verpackt
  sein
quotation
  Angebot

➡ Briefe 64, 65

20 April 20..

Sovereign Assurance Ltd
London Regional Marine Branch
24 Lime Street
LONDON
EC3 7JE

Dear Sirs

Thank you for your quotation of 10 April for ware-house to warehouse cover for a consignment of 50 bales of raw silk from Liverpool to Marseille to be shipped on or after June 1st.

We are pleased to accept your quotation and would request you to forward the necessary documents to us for the policy to be signed.

We have taken note of your stipulation that seaworthy packing is necessary and will ensure that this is provided.

Yours faithfully
TURNPIKE TRADING COMPANY LTD

Ronald Soames
Director

consignment
   Sendung
on or after
   am oder nach dem
quotation
   (Preis-)Angebot
policy   Police
take note of
   zur Kenntnis
   nehmen
stipulation
   hier: Bedingung
seaworthy packing
   seemäßige Ver-
   packung
ensure
   sicherstellen
provide
   besorgen, zur Ver-
   fügung stellen

67 Erneuerung der Abschreibe-Police
Renewal of floating policy

From: Condor.insurance@com.uk
To: PE.timber@network.com.de
Date: 25 May 20..
Subject: Renewal of floating policy No. 896/3/96

Thank you for your letter of May 10th in which you request the above-mentioned floating policy covering shipments of timber from Singapore to UK ports be renewed.

We hereby confirm that warehouse to warehouse cover has once again been provided for by ourselves to the value of £40,000.

Regards
CONDOR INSURANCE (U.K.) LTD

Ralf Barrow
Commercial Policies Division

shipment
 hier: Ladung
timber
 Holz
renew
 erneuern
to the value of
 im Wert von
Commercial Policies Division
 Abteilung für Handelspolicen

12 March 20..

Messrs Porter & Jones
Solicitors
41 Leadbetter Lane
LONDON
EC3 9PP

Dear Sirs

We have pleasure in informing you, as valued customers of long standing, that "Infotec", which has hitherto traded as a sole proprietorship will, as from June 1st of this year, commence trading as a private limited company under the name, "Infotec Ltd".

You may rest assured that the high standard of personal attention and consultancy afforded to our customers in the past will be maintained and, indeed, underpinned by a broader spread of expertise and experience.

Enclosed you will find our "Customer Services" brochure itemising our enhanced range of services and providing biographical details of the new co-directors we have been fortunate enough to have join us.

Please do not hesitate to contact us should you have any queries as regards your firm's requirements or any other matter of concern.

All service contracts extending beyond May 31st will be amended to include the company under its new name and forwarded to our customers for signature.

We look forward to the pleasure of serving you soon.

Yours faithfully
INFOTEC
...

valued customer geschätzter Kunde
of long standing mit langjährigem guten Ruf
hitherto bisher, bis jetzt
sole proprietorship Einzelunternehmen
private limited company (Ltd) (britische) Gesellschaft mit beschränkter Haftung
rest assured versichert sein
underpin unterstützen
a broader spread ein größerer Umfang
expertise Fachwissen, Expertise
range of services Palette der Dienstleistungen
biographical details biographische Einzelheiten
service contract Dienstleistungsvertrag

Britannia Rock Building Society
24–26 Old Cattle Market
Manchester
MA6 7BR

15 April 20..

Mr & Mrs William Galsworthy
42 Acacia Avenue
ROTHERHAM
RO1 4IK

Dear Mr and Mrs Galsworthy

Opening of a New Branch

We have great pleasure in announcing that we shall shortly be opening a new branch of the *Britannia Rock Building Society* within easy reach of your home address.

We are now handling such a large volume of accounts in the north of England that it has proved necessary to expand our activities to cope with the ever-increasing demand for our services.

The new Branch Manager in Rotherham, Mr Terence Birchall, has had many years experience in the field of property acquisition and finance and would welcome an opportunity to meet you personally. He would therefore like to invite you to the new branch's open day on Monday, May 1st between 10 am and 3.30 pm when the *Britannia Rock* will be pleased to extend its hospitality to all visitors caring to participate in light refreshment.

Our Head Office in Manchester, which currently

.../2

branch	Filiale
within easy reach	leicht erreichbar
handle	verwalten
volume	Umfang
account	Konto
prove necessary	sich als notwendig herausstellen
ever-increasing demand	ständig steigende Nachfrage
Branch Manager	Filialleiter
property acquisition	Erwerb von Liegenschaften
hospitality	Gastfreundschaft
participate	teilnehmen
light refreshment	leichte Erfrischung
transfer	übertragen

holds your account, will be sending you our "New Option" form, which will enable you to transfer your account to the Rotherham Branch with a minimum of formalities, should you so wish. Customers opting to retain their account in Manchester are, of course, at liberty to do so. The choice is entirely up to you. For your information we enclose details of some of the new services which will be available at all our branches from the autumn of this year.

We look forward to meeting you in May and would also like to take this opportunity to thank you for the trust you have placed in us in the past.

Yours sincerely
BRITANNIA ROCK BUILDING SOCIETY

Hardy Winter
Chief Executive

Enc

formality
  Formalität
opt wählen
retain behalten
**be at liberty to do
  s.th.** frei wählen
  können etw. zu tun

70 Änderung der Firmenanschrift
Change of firm's address

21 July 20..

Harvard Plastics Ltd
100–110 Heavytree Lane
PENZANCE
PE2 6ZZ

Dear Sir or Madam

Please note that our firm will be trading from a new
address as from August 15 and address all future
correspondence to:-

Trelawney Plastic Moulds Ltd
Units 1–4
Rusholm Bridge Trading Estate
Penzance PE2 8PU

Our telephone and fax numbers as well as our
e-mail adress remain unchanged.

Yours faithfully

P. J. O'Sullivan (Ms)
Communications Manager

note
  hier: zur Kenntnis
  nehmen
trade
  Handel treiben
plastic mould
  Plastikform
trading estate
  Gewerbegebiet
remain unchanged
  unverändert bleiben

1 February 20..

Southall Groceries
42 Clarence Parade
SOUTHALL
MX3 6ZZ

Dear Sirs

It is our sad duty to inform you that for personal reasons The Hackney Trading Company Ltd will be dissolved as from June 1st. This is due to the fact that the principal shareholder and director, Mr Terence Newbury, will be retiring at the end of May and the other members are, for personal reasons, not in a position to take over the running of the company.

The company will be dissolved in the customary manner as prescribed by the Companies Acts (1948–81) with Mr Terence Newbury acting as liquidator for a period of one year.

All outstanding orders will be executed in accordance with existing contracts.

New orders can be placed until March 31 of this year.

We wish to take this opportunity to thank you for the loyalty you have shown towards our company and assure you that we will also be pleased to answer any queries you may have regarding your contracts or any other matters arising.

Yours faithfully
THE HACKNEY TRADING COMPANY LTD
...

dissolve auflösen
principal shareholder Hauptgesellschafter
retire in den Ruhestand gehen
running
 hier: Leitung
customary üblich
prescribe
 vorschreiben
Companies Act
 (britisches) Gesetz zur Regelung des Gesellschaftsrechts
liquidator
 Liquidator, Masseverwalter
outstanding order
 ausstehender Auftrag
existing order
 bestehender Auftrag
loyalty
 Treue, Loyalität
arise sich ergeben, auftauchen

72 Bewerbung um eine Stelle
Job application

➡ Brief 73

15th June 20..

The Manager
Air Space Freight Forwarding
100 Thornbury Road
NEWCASTLE
NO2 6ZE
England

Dear Sir or Madam

I am writing in reply to your advertisement in the European News of June 12th for the post of Sales Manager in your European Division.

I am aged 27, of German nationality, single, bilingual German/English and am currently employed as Freight Co-ordinator with Federal Express (Deutschland) in Düsseldorf where I am responsible for freight movements to and from the US and the UK. I have held this post for three years now and would welcome an opportunity to work in Britain.

I now have a total of 5 years' work experience in freight forwarding, having completed a 2 1/2-year training course as a freight forwarder with Kühne & Nagel, Dortmund, where I stayed for a further two years after completing my training period before taking up my current post at Federal Express. My current performance-related salary is in excess of £30K p.a.

I enclose a full curriculum vitae and the names of two referees as stipulated.

I look forward to your reply at your earliest convenience.

Yours faithfully
...

sales manager Verkaufsleiter
nationality Staatsangehörigkeit
Freight Coordinator Frachtkoordinator
freight movement Frachttransport
welcome an opportunity eine Gelegenheit begrüßen
freight forwarding Frachtversand
freight forwarder Spediteur
performance-related leistungsbezogen
£ 30K p. a. £ 30.000 pro Jahr *(K = 1.000)*
curriculum vitae Lebenslauf
referee *hier:* Auskunftgeber
stipulate festsetzen, verlangen

➡ Brief 72

21 June 20..

Mr Peter Schulz
Alte Bahnhofstr. 100
44892 Bochum
Germany

Dear Mr Schulz

Thank you for your letter of 15 June in which you submit your application for the post of European Division Sales Manager.

Interviews for the post in question are being held in London at the Novotel at Heathrow Airport during the weekend of July 19–20. We are inviting suitable candidates to attend for a preliminary interview on the Saturday. On the Sunday short-listed candidates will then proceed to a second round of interviews conducted by a panel made up of our Human Resources Manager and staff.

All short-listed candidates will be notified approximately 10 days after interview.

Travel and accommodation expenses will be borne by the company for all candidates living outside the UK who are invited to interview.

Please confirm your participation by return, indicating your time of arrival.

Yours sincerely
AIR SPACE FREIGHT FORWARDING

Henry Fuller
Human Resources Division

European Division
  Unternehmens-
  bereich Europa
preliminary
  vorläufig
short-listed
  in die engere Wahl
  gekommen
proceed fortfah-
  ren, weiterkommen
panel Ausschuss,
  Kommission
human resources
  hier: Personalabtei-
  lung
staff Belegschaft
notify
  benachrichtigen
participation
  Teilnahme
time of arrival
  Ankunftszeit

3rd April 20..

To whom it may concern

Ms. MARIA SCHNELL

Ms Schnell worked with Technology Transfer Systems Ltd. as Departmental Head in our software development and documentation department during the period from 1 January 19.. to 31 March 20..

After having rapidly taken stock of the resources available in this department, both in terms of manpower and technology, she was able to proceed to evaluating its strengths and weaknesses. Her restructuring of the section led to an immediate improvement in morale and performance resulting in greater efficiency and dedication from all concerned.

The areas for which she took responsibility involved many skills: documenting, typing and layout of a user manual, testing the software system during development and liaising with software engineers as bugs or queries were raised.

Her ability to chair meetings and conduct them in a manner conducive to constructive results has proved invaluable in the course of her three years with our company.

Technology Transfer Systems Ltd will sadly miss the skills and dedication of which Ms Schnell's departure will deprive the company. We do not hesitate to recommend her to any future employer.

Yours faithfully
...

to whom it may concern *etwa:* an alle, die es angeht (bei englischen Zeugnissen oft verwendete Überschrift)
departmental head Abteilungsleiter
software development Softwareentwicklung
take stock Bestandsaufnahme machen
resource *hier:* Mittel
manpower (verfügbare) Arbeitskraft
efficiency Leistungsfähigkeit
dedication *hier:* Engagement
user manual Benutzerhandbuch
liaise Verbindung halten
bug *hier:* Defekt
chair den Vorsitz führen
conducive to dienlich zu, förderlich für

110

September 15, 20..

Mr Jens Grünewald
Rombacher Hütte 93
44795 Bochum
Germany

Dear Mr Grünewald:

Thank you for your letter of September 1, in which you apply for the post of European Sales Coordinator.

Having studied your résumé, references and testimonials we have come to the conclusion that your particular area of expertise lies in transport logistics and human resources management. What we are looking for, however, is a candidate who is an advertising and marketing specialist. For this reason we are unable to offer you the post in question.

As we feel that your skills could be used elsewhere in our European operation, we have passed your application on to our European Transport Dept., where it will be put on file pending a future vacancy.

With best wishes for the future,

Sincerely,
INTERNATIONAL ELECTRONICS INC

Benjamin Rhodes
Personnel Manager

European Sales Coordinator Europäischer Verkaufskoordinator
résumé Lebenslauf
testimonial Zeugnis
transport logistics Transportlogistik
human resources management Personalführung
advertising specialist Werbefachmann
put on file in die Unterlagen kommen, ablegen
pending a future vacancy bis zu einer zukünftigen Vakanz
Personnel Manager Leiter der Personalabteilung

3 February 20..

National Chiswick Bank Ltd
Chiswick High Road Branch
27 Chiswick High Road
Chiswick
LONDON
W4T 6PP
England

For the attention of the Manager

Dear Sir or Madam

As our company has enjoyed excellent relations with your bank in the past we would be most grateful if you could assist our newly appointed Market Research Co-ordinator (U.K. Division), Herr Franz Lahusen, on his arrival in London at the beginning of next month.

He has been entrusted with the task of drawing up energy consumption profiles for major energy users in the process engineering sector in the south of England and would therefore appreciate any assistance your bank can give him as regards potential customers and their suitability. We feel that your wide experience in dealing with corporate customers and the considerable skill with which you have handled our affairs in the past will greatly aid Herr Lahusen in this undertaking.

We wish to take this opportunity to extend our thanks to you in advance for any assistance given to him in this matter and remain,

Yours faithfully
GEA Energietechnik GmbH
...

excellent relation ausgezeichnete Beziehung
newly appointed neu ernannt
market research Marktforscher
draw up entwerfen, erstellen
energy consumption profile Energieverbrauchsprofil
process engineering Fertigungsplanung
potential customer möglicher Kunde
suitability Eignung
corporate customer Firmenkunde
undertaking Vorhaben
extend *hier:* ausdrücken

Europlast AG
Baubergerstr. 28
80992 München
Germany
E-mail: europlast.ag@germanet.de

31 March 20..

New Channel Ltd
Unit 6
Hadrian Industrial Estate
CAMBRIDGE
CA4 9UJ
England

Dear Mr Rogers

Our New Representive, Mr Arnold Klein

We are pleased to inform you that, as from May 1st of this year, Mr Arnold Klein will be our new representative in the south of England. He will be taking over from Mr Friedrich Schäfer, who will be returning to Germany for a post of responsibility in Eastern Germany.

Mr Klein will be moving to the UK after a highly successful spell in Canada where he represented our interests from January 20.. to March 20... In the course of his employment with our company, Mr Klein has been able to amass an enviable amount of knowledge as regards local market requirements and customers' expectations and his sound technical background has enabled him to diagnose customer needs quickly and accurately.

You may rest assured that the high standard of service you have come to expect from our company

.../2

spell
  hier: Aufenthalt
represent interests
  Interessen vertreten
employment
  Beschäftigungszeit
amass sammeln
enviable
  beneidenswert
as regards
  bezüglich
**local market re-
  quirements** lokale
  Marktbedürfnisse
**customers' expecta-
  tions** Erwartun-
  gen der Kunden
sound
  hier: fundiert
**technical back-
  ground**
  technisches Hinter-
  grundwissen
customer needs
  Kundenbedürfnisse
high standard
  hohes Niveau

will remain available to all our customers and that all contracts, agreements and arrangements between yourselves and our organisation will in no way be affected by the new appointment.

Mr Klein will be calling upon you in the near future to introduce himself personally and is looking forward to meeting our existing business partners and also expanding our operation in the UK.

Should you have any queries as regards future arrangements we will be pleased to provide you with any information you may require.

Yours sincerely
EUROPLAST AG

Peter Wirt
European Sales Co-ordinator

arrangement
  Vereinbarung
appointment *hier:*
  Stellenbesetzung
call upon s.o.
  j-n. besuchen
introduce oneself
  sich vorstellen
operation
  hier: Tätigkeitsfeld

114

NRW Frachtenkontor
Blumenstraße 23–27
44147 Dortmund
Germany
E-mail: NRWfracht@vorm.de

15 April 20..

Balcombes Insurance Loss Assessor,
Surveyors and Valuers
2 Paradise Row
LONDON
E2 4PB
England

Dear Sirs

Vehicle Damage and Part-Loss of Load

Please assess the costs arising from the damage
to our vehicle Reg. No. DO-KA 385 and its load
(motor vehicle components) when it was involved
in an accident with an oncoming lorry on the approach road to Dover Eastern Docks on April 12th.

The vehicle and the remaining part of the load were
recovered by:

Crowvale Haulage Ltd
(Commerical Vehicle Recovery Services)
Silverdale House
Pump Lane
London W5 7UJ

Tel. 0181 573 2624

at whose premises they can be examined during
usual working hours by appointment.

.../2

Surveyor
  hier: (technischer)
  Gutachter
Valuer Taxator
vehicle damage
  Fahrzeugschaden
part-loss
  Teilverlust
load Ladung
**motor vehicle com-
  ponent**
  Kraftfahrzeugteil
oncoming
  entgegenkommend
approach road
  Zugangsstraße
recover
  hier: bergen
haulage
  (Lkw-)Transport
**commercial vehicle
  recovery service**
  Bergungsdienst für
  Nutzfahrzeuge
**usual working
  hours** normale
  Arbeitszeit

115

The Dover Constabulary has made a report on the accident and an investigation into the collision is being conducted by Detective Constable Ralf Hayes.

We also enclose on a separate sheet from our insurers, Star Insurance, a list of points which should be considered in your report.

Please submit your report and invoice in triplicate to ourselves as soon as possible to enable us to make a claim to our insurers.

Yours faithfully
NRW Frachtenkontor

Harald Schmidt
Transport Manager

Enc

by appointment
  nach Vereinbarung
collision
  Zusammenstoß
detective constable
  Kriminalwacht-
  meister
invoice Rechnung
in triplicate
  3fach, in 3facher
  Ausfertigung

Prendergast & Johnson
Investment Consultants
52 Carter Lane
London EC2 6ZG
England

FG/FB
10 February 20..

IBA Investmentfonds GmbH
Hohe Brück 44
60437 Frankfurt am Main
Germany

Dear Mr Kaltwasser

Current UK Stock Market Trends

Telecom issues were popular yesterday helping prevent a sharp reversal in the FTSE 100. For this reason investors used the opportunity of a firm London market to buy into a sector that has seen some of the biggest falls over the last four weeks.

The news that Deutsche Telekom is considering floating its on-line and mobile telecom interests reassured investors. Speaking soon after the company had announced a fall in interim profits, the chairman said the group's T-Online and T-Mobil units could be sold off within six months, with Deutsche Telekom retaining a majority stake in the companies.

In London much of the buying interest was in Brit-Com, the market's second biggest company. The shares, whose 12-month high was £11.51, have underperformed the FTSE All-Share by 6 per cent in the last month and 9 per cent in the last three months.

.../2

stock market trend Trend am Aktienmarkt
issues Emissionen
reversal Umschwung
FTSE 100 Financial Times Stock Exchange 100 (Index für die 100 führenden Aktien)
firm market fester Markt
buy into sich einkaufen in
float floaten, begeben
reassure beruhigen
interim profit Zwischengewinn
retain behalten
majority stake mehrheitlicher Anteil
12-month high Höchststand seit 12 Monaten
underperform nicht erreichen

However, as a result of considerable demand yesterday they bounced back over the £10 mark, closing 56 ahead at £10.04.

In the rest of the sector, Sinergy Telecom rose 60 to £13.33 while Pocketfone appreciated by 36 to £12.33. Barabus was also in demand, the shares adding 40 to £12.52, with buying interest also encouraged by a recommendation from Dresdner Kleinwort Benson.

Hard-pressed mortgage banks Northern Stone and Dewsbury & Pickering jumped 37 ½ to 851 ½ p and 29 to 698 p, with added impetus from continued optimism about the housing market, particularly in the south-east.

Investment management group HarveyPlus gained 10 to 543 ½ p after one broker recommended the stock because of "on track" second-quarter results.

We feel that this is a good time to investigate Telecom stock with a view to a substantial commitment in the medium term. However, we recommend you exercise caution until the Deutsche Telekom flotation has been completed.

Should there be any last-minute developments we will e-mail you immediately.

Yours sincerely
PRENDERGAST & JOHNSON
...

bounce back zurückschnellen
close abschließen
appreciate hier: steigen
hard-pressed unter Druck stehend
mortgage bank Hypothekenbank
added impetus zusätzlicher Auftrieb
gain hier: zulegen
"on track" results hier: erwartete Ergebnisse
with a view to mit Aussicht auf
commitment hier: Engagement
exercise caution Vorsicht üben

August 17, 20..

Hitech Software Inc.
400 Sunnyvale Boulevard
San José CA 94021
USA

Ladies and Gentlemen:

<u>Our Order of 1 August for 10 Site Licenses for Software Application</u>

We refer to our above-mentioned order for site licenses for your Megamerge application and wish to point out that, at the time of placing our order, Megamerge 3.0 was the latest version commercially available. As you have since brought out Megamerge 3.1 we wish to amend our order accordingly, as we only install state-of-the-art software.

We trust this amendment will not bring about any delay in delivery. Should this be the case please fax us immediately.

Sincerely yours,
ZIMMERMANN INFORMATIK

Jens Zimmermann
Proprietor

site license Anlagen-, Systemlizenz
software application Softwareanwendung
at the time of placing our order zum Zeitpunkt unserer Auftragsvergabe
commercially available im Handel erhältlich
amend ändern
state-of-the-art dem neuesten Stand der Technik entsprechend
bring about mit sich bringen
Proprietor Firmeninhaber

HJ/klt
19 July 20..

Europhar International Ltd
115 Gloucester Road
LONDON
W4 3HH
England

<u>Attn: Mr William Mason, Export Sales Manager</u>

Dear Mr Mason

<u>Our Order No. 73F/93 Disposable Syringes
of 10 July 20..</u>

With reference to the above-mentioned order we
wish to change the quantity required from 10,000
as originally stated to 15,000 disposable syringes.

We trust you will be able to accommodate us in
this matter and assume that the conditions agreed
still apply.

Please confirm this amendment in writing, stating
any change in delivery date. We are willing to accept two part-deliveries (e.g. of 10,000 and 5,000
units) should this prove necessary.

Yours sincerely

Harald Jung
Purchasing Manager

disposable syringe
  Wegwerfspritze
as originally stated
  wie ursprünglich
  angegeben
accommodate
  entgegenkommen
apply
  hier: gültig sein
amendment
  Änderung
delivery date
  Lieferdatum
part-delivery
  Teillieferung
unit Stück, Einheit
Purchasing Manager
  Einkaufsleiter

12 August 20..

Riverside Organ Studios
50 Station Road
NEW MALDEN
KT1 R55
England

Dear Mr Marshall

We confirm receipt of your order for two Vox Z1 47
synthesisers but regret having to inform you that
Vox Ltd have now gone out of business – thus
making it impossible for us to accept your order.

There is a wide variety of similar instruments on
the UK market, however, and for your information
we enclose our latest catalogue and price list.

At present orders for the instruments listed can be
processed within 4 weeks of receipt of order.

Assuring you of our best attention at all times we
remain,

Yours sincerely

Terry Webb
Export Sales

confirm receipt
den Erhalt
bestätigen
synthesiser
Synthesizer
go out of business
das Geschäft
aufgeben
wide variety
große Vielfalt
instrument
Instrument
process an order
einen Auftrag
abwickeln
**4 weeks of receipt
of order**
4 Wochen nach
Auftragseingang

11 July 20..

PLANCO LTD
16 Garden Avenue
HARWICH
CO12 4JR
Great Britain

Attn: Ms Anne Howard, Accounts

Dear Ms Howard

Your statement of account no. 5471 of 30 June 20..

Enclosed please find a copy of your statement up to and including 30th June 20.. showing a balance of € 230.00 in your favour.

Unfortunately, we think there is a mistake in this statement. You have forgotten to credit us with € 50.00, a reduction which you granted us on 5th May 20.. because one case of your delivery covering order no. 3099 arrived here in damaged condition.

Please check this statement again and if you agree with it we shall be pleased to receive your corrected version. We shall then remit the amount of € 180.00 immediately to your account by banker's transfer.

Yours sincerely
Sellhuber & Maier GmbH
...

statement of account   Kontoauszug
balance   Saldo
credit   gutschreiben
reduction   Nachlass
grant   gewähren
covering   *hier:* betreffend, abdeckend
in damaged condition   in beschädigtem Zustand
corrected version   korrigierte, verbesserte Version
remit   überweisen, schicken
by banker's transfer   durch Banküberweisung

13 Feb 20..

Thailand Timber Company
Wireless Road
Bangkok
Thailand

Dear Sir or Madam

We have received the B/L and insurance certificate for the consignment of 50 tons of palletised teak on board m.v. "August Moon", which is due to dock in Liverpool at the end of this month.

We note with dismay, however, that the Bs/L include the notation "6 pallets damaged". As you well know, our company sells timber "on water" to European importers and an unclean B/L is only negotiable in exceptional cases. We fail to understand why you did not provide the shipping company with a letter of indemnity as soon as it was apparent that the goods were not in perfect condition.

It only remains to be hoped that the damage is to the pallets and not to the timber. Should the consignment prove unsaleable we will review all future contracts with your company and seek redress for the loss of trade.

Yours faithfully
NORTHERN TIMBER LTD

J. B. Jones
Manager

B/L = bill of lading
  Konnossement
insurance certificate
  Versicherungszertifikat
consignment
  Sendung
palletised teak
  palettisiertes Teakholz
m.v. = motor vessel
  Motorschiff
notation
  Vermerk, Notierung
pallet   Palette
unclean B/L
  unreines Konossement
shipping company
  Reederei
letter of indemnity
  Ausfallbürgschaft
unsaleable
  unverkäuflich
seek redress
  Wiedergutmachung suchen

85 Zahlung per Postüberweisung
Payment by Mail Payment Order

From: Finchley trading@com.uk
To: sri.lanka.tea@radio.com
Date: 25 February 20..
Subject: Our order of May 15, 20..

Dear Mr Patel

We confirm receipt of the 30 chests of Ceylon
Pekoe tea ordered by ourselves on May 15th.

As agreed in the Contract of Sale we instructed
the Finchley Branch of the Benson Bank to arrange
for payment by Mail Payment Order through your
bank in Colombo. Instructions to this effect were
mailed to Sri Lanka today and we have been given
to understand that you will receive payment in
approximately a fortnight's time.

We look forward to doing further business with you
in the near future and remain,

Yours sincerely
FINCHLEY TRADING COMPANY

Daljit Singh
General Manager

chest Kiste
contract of sale
 Verkaufsvertrag
instruct
 anweisen
branch
 Filiale
arrange for
 payment
 die Zahlung
 veranlassen
instructions to this
 effect
 diesbezügliche
 Anweisungen
give to understand
 zu verstehen geben

March 3rd, 20..

Messrs Miller & Smutts
95-101 East London Roads
Pietermaritzburg
South Africa

For the attention of Mr Ronald Miller

Dear Mr Miller

Advice of Draft re Your Order No. JK8/3/93 for
Agricultural Sprinklers

In accordance with the above-mentioned order the
3 irrigation systems ordered have been shipped on
board m.v. "Anastasia", CIF Durban. The vessel is
due to dock in Durban at the end of this month.

We enclose the following documents:-

Commercial Invoice
Customs Invoice
Copy of B/L

The Durban branch of Benson International will
release the original Bs/L and the Insurance Certificate upon acceptance of our draft drawn upon
yourselves at 30 d/s.

We trust the sprinklers will arrive punctually and in
good condition and look forward to the opportunity
of serving you in the future.

Yours sincerely
KÖHLER BEWÄSSERUNGSANLAGEN GmbH
...

agricultural sprinkler
landwirtschaftliche Berieselungsanlage
irrigation system
Bewässerungs-system
CIF = cost, insur-ance, freight
(Incoterm)
commercial invoice
Handelsrechnung, Handelsfaktura
customs invoice
Zollrechnung, Zoll-faktura
copy of B/L = bill of lading   Kopie des Konnossements
insurance certificate
Versicherungszer-tifikat
draft
Tratte, Wechsel
at 30 d/s = days/sight
auf 30 Tage Sicht

The Steel Box Company Ltd
Smithington Lane
Smithington
Sheffield SH7 4AG
England
e-mail: steel.box@netcom.co.uk

TH/oq
27 February 20..

TGH Bleche Handelsgesellschaft mbH
Rombacher Hütte 99
44795 Bochum
Germany

Dear Sirs

Outstanding Balances Due to your Company to Date

We regret to inform you that the current worldwide recession in the steel industry has led to a collapse in the market for viably priced metal boxes made in Europe. The sad fact of the matter ist that Eastern European and Far Eastern competitors have flooded our traditional sales territory with good-quality products at 75% of our rock-bottom prices.

We, ourselves, are unable to meet our financial obligations with respect to our bankers and suppliers, with the consequence that insolvency proceedings in accordance with the UK Insolvency Act of 1986 have been instituted against us by our first-ranking creditor, Benson Bank Plc.

The liquidator appointed will wind up our company and pay preferential and secured creditors in full. Thereafter, non-prefential trading creditors such as

...../2

outstanding balance ausstehender Saldo
worldwide recession weltweite Rezession
steel industry Stahlbranche
viably priced metal boxes Metallkästen zu durchsetzbaren Preisen
Far Eastern competitor fernöstliche Konkurrenten
sales territory Verkaufsgebiet
rock-bottom price allerniedrigster Preis
insolvency proceedings Vergleichsverfahren
Insolvency Act Insolvenzgesetz
institute einleiten
first-ranking creditor an 1. Stelle stehender Gläubiger

yourselves with unsecured debts will be taken into consideration.

You will be informed in due course of the date of creditors' meeting, which all parties concerned will be invited to attend.

We hope you will appreciate that we are the victims of a situation entirely beyond our control and would stress the fact that we have been given assurances that the liquidator will treat all creditors equitably.

Yours faithfully
THE STEEL BOX COMPANY LTD

Terence Hill
Company Secretary

wind up   auflösen, liquidieren
preferential creditor   Vorzugsgläubiger
unsecured debts   nicht gesicherte (ungedeckte) Schulden
victim   Opfer
beyond our control   außerhalb unserer Kontrolle
equitably   unparteiisch

2 April 20..

Carpendale Wholesale Grocery Supplies Ltd
Unit 6
Highgate Trading Estate
LONDON
N8 9IP

Dear Sirs

We regret to inform you that the recent opening and proximity of a new branch of the "Cash & Carry Supergreen" greengrocer's chain has led to a disastrous decline in the trading situation of our business. This, in turn, has resulted in our no longer being able to meet our current and long-term financial obligations.

Our preferential creditors have obtained a receiving order, under the provisions of which we have been granted a month's grace, during which time we have the opportunity to reach an amicable settlement with our non-preferential creditors. Should we not achieve voluntary composition, the court will issue an adjudication order and appoint a trustee to take charge of liquidating our assets.

We would therefore respectfully invite you to attend the creditors' meeting which will take place on April 15 next on our premises.

You may rest assured that each application will be treated on its merits and in good faith.

Yours faithfully
QUICK TURNOVER GREENGROCERIES LTD

Harold Archer
Chief Accountant

wholesale
 Großhandel
grocery supplies
 Lebensmittelliefe-
 rungen
trading estate
 Gewerbegebiet
trading situation
 Geschäftslage
**preferential
creditor**
 Vorzugsgläubiger
receiving order
 Konkurseröffnungs-
 beschluss
provision
 Vorkehrung
**an amicable settle-
ment** eine freund-
 schaftliche Einigung
**voluntary compo-
sition** ein freiwil-
 liger Vergleich
adjudication
 richterliche Ent-
 scheidung (*über
 Konkurseröffnung*)
trustee
 Treuhänder, *hier:*
 Konkursverwalter

Auftrag auf Aktienkauf
Order for shares

➡ Brief 90

14 May 20..

SouthWestern Investment Centre
PO Box 205
WATFORD
DW1 1BP
England

Portfolio No.: D/281248-2-93

Dear Sir or Madam

Please buy positions in the following shares in accordance with the limits indicated. A total value of £15,000 should not be exceeded.

a) TCC Shares	to the value of € 5,000
b) EuroRoad Shares	to the value of € 1,000
c) PowerGen	to the value of € 9,000
(rights issue as per allotment letter)	
	Total € 15,000

Please debit the appropriate amount to my South-Western Investor Account.

Yours faithfully

G. P. Courtney (Dr)

portfolio
Portefeuille
share Aktie
total value
Gesamtwert
exceed
übersteigen
rights issue
Bezugsrechts-
emission
allotment letter
Zuteilungsbrief
debit belasten
appropriate
amount
entsprechender
Betrag
investor account
Investorenkonto

90

➡ Brief 89

30 June 20..

Dr G. P. Courtney
Trantenrother Weg 56
58455 Witten
Germany

Portfolio No.: D/281248-2-93

Dear Dr Courtney

PORTFOLIO VALUATION STATEMENT

We are pleased to forward as per the enclosed
your Portfolio statement for the first half of 20..

The statement itemises your current investments,
their original cost and current market price, their
yield and the total value of your holdings. The
Contract Notes from share deals concluded in the
course of the last week are also enclosed.

All profits accruing have been credited to your
SouthWestern Investor Account, which currently
shows a net balance of € 17,789.95 in your favour.

We look forward to serving you in the future and
remain,

Yours sincerely
SOUTHWESTERN INVESTMENT CENTRE

P. K. Hodgkith
Portfolio Manager

Encs

portfolio valuation
  Portefeuillebewer-
  tung
current investment
  laufende Investition
market price
  Marktpreis
yield Ertrag
holdings
  hier: Besitz
contract note
  Effektenkauf- bzw.
  Verkaufsabrech-
  nung
share deal
  Aktiengeschäft
accruing profit
  auflaufender
  Gewinn
credit gutschreiben
net balance
  Nettosaldo
Portfolio Manager
  Portefeuille-Mana-
  ger

Lowndes Lambert
Trading Group
Bullrush Lane
London E3 8JL

GL/bk
9 June 20..

Hartmann & Ibing
Warenarbitrage
Alsterberg 95
22335 Hamburg
Germany

Dear Sirs

We are currently involved in a dispute with the Schmitt Handelsgesellschaft GmbH, Hamburg, who have refused payment for a consignment of 4,000 sacks of robusta coffee from São Paulo in Brazil. The consignment is currently on board m.v. "Polixenes" in Hamburg.

They maintain, after having taken samples, that the quality of the coffee does not correspond to the description "best quality" as stated in the contract and have appointed an arbitrator to act on their behalf. The company representing their interests is Gebrüder Sohn, Warenarbitrage, in Hamburg. A copy of their report is enclosed.

Our contract with Schmitt provides for arbitrage in Hamburg and for our arbitrator to be notified of the name of Schmitt's arbitrator within 7 days of appointment. In addition, all arbitrators are to be members of the Chamber of Commerce in the city in which the parties involved have registered their companies.

...../2

dispute	Streitfall
consignment	Sendung
m.v. = motor vessel	Motorschiff
take samples	Muster (Proben) nehmen
appoint	bestimmen, ernennen
arbitrator	Schiedsmann
act on their behalf	um für sie tätig zu werden
provide for	vorsehen
within 7 days of appointment	innerhalb von 7 Tagen nach Ernennung
the parties involved	die beteiligten Parteien
register	eintragen

We would therefore be most grateful if you would act as our arbitrator in this matter. We are of the opinion that the quality of the consignment of coffee in question is well within the limits of the definition "best quality" and would request you to take samples from a large cross-section of the sacks making up the consignment.

We trust you will succeed in upholding our claim in this matter, thus obviating the need for an umpire to be appointed.

Yours faithfully
Lowndes Lambert Trading Group

Gerald Lambert
Director

Enc

be well within the limits durchaus innerhalb der Grenzen liegen
cross-section Querschnitt
make up *hier:* bilden
uphold (unter-)stützen
obviate zuvorkommen, verhindern
umpire Obmann, Schiedsmann

23 August 20..

Dear Customer

Thank you for your enquiry regarding our products. We enclose a current brochure outlining our entire range and will be most pleased to assist you further with your choice of vehicle.

The content of the brochure enclosed is as accurate as possible from information available at the time of going to press. Dimensions, weights and plan drawings are approximate. Leisureworld Caravans (U.K.) Ltd. reserves the right to alter specifications, colours, models and ranges as materials and conditions demand and, consequently, can accept no responsibility for discrepancies between information contained in this brochure and subsequent models. This brochure, therefore, does not constitute an offer by Leisureworld Caravans (U.K.) Ltd.

If, after having studied our sales literature, you require further information, please do not hesitate to contact one of our approved dealers in the U.K., all of whose names, addresses, telephone and fax numbers as well as e-mail addresses are enclosed.

We look forward to the pleasure of serving you in the near future.

Yours sincerely
Leisureworld Caravans (U.K.) Ltd.

Harvey Threadgold
General Manager

Encs

outline *hier:* einen Überblick geben
range (Produkt-)Palette
choice Wahl
dimension Abmessung
plan drawing Planzeichnung
reserve the right sich das Recht vorbehalten
alter abändern
consequently infolgedessen
accept responsibility Verantwortung übernehmen
discrepancy Abweichung
subsequent nachfolgend
constitute bilden, darstellen
sales literature Verkaufsmaterial
approved dealer anerkannter Händler

Newtown Electronics
36 Barton Road
Hatfield
Herts HT9 7PQ

28 March 20..

Messrs Cotton, Gummersall & Palmer
Windsor House
1008 East End Road
LONDON
SW16 7UJ

Dear Sirs

<u>Breach of Contract due to Delay in Delivery</u>

We are writing to you to request you to represent our interests in what we consider to be a clear case of breach of contract.

From the correspondence enclosed you will note that "DV-Electronic Data Systems Deutschland GmbH" have failed to comply with the terms set out in our Contract of Sale (see enclosure), whereby delivery of the goods in question (viz 400 VGA Monitors, Type MultiSync XL) was assured by 15th January 20..

We finally took delivery of these articles on March 10th, by which time we had incurred considerable financial losses and were obliged to supply our customers at 25% under list price.
We have already deducted out losses from the invoice amount + 10% administration charges and transferred the amended invoice amount to DV-Electronic's account. We have, in addition, can-

.../2

breach of contract	Vertragsbruch
delay in delivery	Lieferverzug
data system	Datensystem
set out	darlegen
the goods in question	die infrage stehenden Güter
viz	nämlich, das heißt
assure	zusichern
be obliged	gezwungen sein
at 25% under list-price	25% unter dem Listenpreis
deduct out	abziehen
invoice amount	Rechnungsbetrag
administration charges	Verwaltungsgebühren

celled a further order (see enclosures) for 400 keyboards. DV-Electronic, however, are insisting upon a list-price settlement and have indicated that they will not accept our cancellation. They have also passed the matter on to their solicitors, who have threatened litigation, should we fail to honour our order for the keyboards.

We welcome your comments on this matter and would be most grateful if you could act in such a manner as to convince DV-Electronic that any further attempt to press their claim would prove futile.

Yours faithfully
NEWTOWN ELECTRONICS

J. B. Butterson
Managing Director

Encs

pass the matter on to their solicitors
die Sache an ihre Rechtsanwälte weiterleiten

threaten litigation
mit einem Rechtsstreit drohen

honour an order
einen Auftrag erfüllen

94 Bestellung eines Management Consultant
Enlisting the aid of a management consultant

20 July 20..

Messrs Price Waterhouse
Management Consultants
Knightsbridge House
185 Knightsbridge
LONDON
SW7 90L

Dear Sirs

As a result of the lasting effects of the current recession, which has affected business badly in our field, we are now obliged to restructure our operation and will have no alternative but to retrench heavily.

We therefore require assistance with the shedding of workers by natural wastage or voluntary redundancy, severance pay, early retirement plans with or without a gratuity, redundancy schemes with retraining opportunities for younger workers and a public relations strategy to help make these inevitable measures more palatable to our employees and the public at large.

In addition, we will need to scrutinize our middle and upper management structures in order to weed out under-productive staff. Here, we will require assistance with assessment procedures to gauge performance and also with the implementation of decisions resulting from the discovery that particular individuals can no longer remain in our employ.

We would therefore request you to contact us immediately with a view to drawing up a profile of our company and putting forward short and medium-term strategies.

Yours faithfully
...

retrench kürzen, sich einschränken
shed workers Arbeitskräfte abbauen
natural wastage natürlicher Abgang
voluntary redundancy freiwillige Freisetzung
severance pay Abfindungszahlung
early retirement plan Frühpensionierungsplan
gratuity Abfindungssumme
palatable schmackhaft
scrutinize gründlich prüfen
weed out aussondern
under-productive staff weniger produktives Personal
assessment procedures Bewertungsverfahren
gauge performance Leistung messen
implementation Einführung

136

June 25, 20..

Constance Cummings
Cosmetics Manufacturers
One World Trade Center
Suite 7691
New York, NY 10048
U.S.A.

Ladies and Gentlemen:

We are now in a position to provide you with the first results of our market survey on German consumer habits as regards the use of cosmetics.

Our field-workers conducted a representative survey of females aged 15–60 years and completed a questionnaire with the test persons on their preferences as regards hair and skin preparations. Our survey incorporated questions on the recycling of packaging, vivisection issues and a possible multi-cultural image of society. In addition, we asked questions on matters such as manufacturing methods and the sourcing of ingredients used for beauty preparations (low-wage labor in the Third World, Amazon rain forest depletion, "natural" and "green" products, herbal remedies, cosmetic substances used by ancient cultures etc.).

Our conclusions and recommendations are set out in detail in the charts included with this letter.

In essence, we recommend that the 15–25 year-old age group be approached with explicit reference to environmentally friendly products, developed on human test subjects and in no way involving the use of animals. Here a synthesis should be a-

…/2

market survey
  Marktstudie
consumer habit
  Verbrauchergewohnheit
questionnaire
  Fragebogen
incorporate
  beinhalten
packaging
  Verpackung
vivisection issue
  Thema der Vivisektion
multi-cultural image of society
  multikulturelles Image der Gesellschaft
manufacturing method Herstellungsmethode
ingredient
  Bestandteil
the Third World
  die Dritte Welt
Amazon rain forest depletion
  Raubbau am Regenwald des Amazonasgebiets

chieved between fashion-consciousness and "natural" beauty. We suggest using both European and African models in harmonious but also dynamic and exciting situations in your advertising.

The 25–40 year-olds will probably best respond to an "enlightened" and realistic approach to the problems of "getting the best out of your looks" with a little help from cosmetics. Here, an "intimate" approach is important, i.e. the cosmetic industry is secretly helping you to enhance your looks, whilst unsuspecting males think it's natural (hair rinses, skin toners, anti-wrinkle preparations).

The 45–60 year-olds will probably best respond to even more subtle allusions to the need for nature to be helped along a little, but here we recommend the idea of, "Go on, enjoy yourself now," or, "Treat yourself to something really good!" Prices for this age group can be increased by 5%–10% to underline market segmentation.

We trust you will be able to incorporate our suggestions in your advertising campaign and will be pleased to clarify any of our findings, should you request us to do so.

Sincerely yours,
DAWSON & DAWSON

A. P. Schleifer
Senior Consultant

Encs

herbal remedy
pflanzliche Arznei
fashion-consciousness Modebewusstsein
enhance (vorteilhaft) zur Geltung bringen
hair rinse
Haarspülung
skin toner
Hauttönungsmittel
anti-wrinkle preparation
Antifaltenpräparat
allusion Anspielung, Hinweis

➡ Brief 97

HARVARD PLASTICS INC.
Broadway
New York, N.Y. 10018
USA
e-mail: HVplastics@aol.com

August 10, 20..

Human Resources Department
Harvard Plastics Inc. (U.K.)
Bull Ring Industrial Estate
BIRMINGHAM
BI8 9LL
United Kingdom

Ladies and Gentlemen:

<u>European Languages Drive</u>

As President of Harvard Plastics Inc. I take great pleasure in utilizing this opportunity to address all operatives in the Human Resources Departments of our European subsidiaries. As you all know, the course of history has brought about momentous changes in Europe and we cannot afford to let new chances pass us by. For this reason, we must all re-think, re-structure and react.

To this end I am issuing a Management Directive to all Human Resources Departments to launch an all-out effort to attract multi-lingual personnel at all levels. The logistics at local level are entirely the province of individual Human Resources Managers, but let me make myself clear on this, we need and expect results and an up-to-date profile of all sub-sidiaries will be drawn up exactly one year from now.

...../2

drive Kampagne, Werbefeldzug
operative *hier:* Angestellter
Human Resources Department Personalabteilung
management directive Managementrichtlinie
an all-out effort eine ganz gewaltige Anstrengung
multi-lingual personnel mehrsprachiges Personal
an up-to-date profile ein auf den neuesten Stand gebrachtes Profil

Existing employees must be encouraged to develop their language skills in their free time in courses run on company premises. Promotion prospects will be made dependent on this. Harvard Plastics are willing to refund employees' outlay on language tuition upon successful completion of a recognised qualification. Extra bonuses will be paid if an employee learns more than one foreign language. Furthermore, additional financial incentives will be made available to promote the study of Eastern European Languages such as Russian, Polish and Hungarian, for I feel that a sales thrust eastwards in the near future can only succeed if our personnel can operate through the medium of the language in the sales territory targeted.

I trust that our European Languages Drive Project will be crowned with success and feel sure that a high degree of response throughout our organization will serve to secure jobs in the future.

Sincerely yours,

Clarence C. Pollock
PRESIDENT

language skill
Sprachfertigkeit
free time Freizeit
company premises
Firmenräume
promotion prospects
Beförderungsaus-
sichten
employees' outlay
Ausgaben der An-
gestellten
language tuition
Sprachunterricht
**recognised quali-
fication** aner-
kannte Qualifikation
sales thrust
Verkaufsvorstoß
sales territory
Verkaufsgebiet

➡ Brief 96

Harvard Plastics Inc. (UK)
Bull Ring Industrial Estate
Birmingham BI8 9LL
United Kingdom
e-mail: HVplastics@aol.com

4th July 20..

The President
Harvard Plastics Inc.
Broadway
New York, NY 10018
USA

Dear Mr Pollock

We have studied your Annual Report for 19.. and come to the conclusion that the loss in pre-tax profits of $1.2bn incurred by Harvard Plastics world-wide was mainly attributable to high labour costs and import duty on plastics entering Europe.

The conclusion we have come to is that relocation of part of your manufacturing facilities in one of the cheaper EU countries (UK, Ireland, Portugal, Greece) may be the answer to import duties, for in this way the "80% local content" ruling as regards goods manufactured by companies in non-EU ownership can be complied with. Over 1,000 Japanese companies already have a production site in the UK alone.

We feel that every effort should be made to contact the municipalities in areas designated by the EU as "regional development areas" in order to obtain EU funding and low-priced land. We are convinced that any effort to bring jobs to Europe will be warmly welcomed by the government and local population

...../2

annual report
Jahresbericht
loss in pre-tax profits Verlust bei den Vor-Steuer-Gewinnen
bn = billion
Milliarde
incur auftreten
relocation
Verlegung
manufacturing facilities Herstellungsbetriebe
the 80% local content ruling
die Regelung, dass 80% aus heimischer Produktion stammen müssen
municipality
städtische Behörde
designate
bezeichnen
regional development area
regionales Entwicklungsgebiet

concerned, with good chances of highly favourable tax relief arrangements for an initial period and, especially in the UK, a pool of skilled labour available immediately.

Our Public Relations Department has already started to sound out local authorities in suitable areas in the UK and we will be sending you a report of our findings in good time for your AGM on 1 September.

You may rest assured that our recommendations will remain confidential, until such time as the matter of relocation in Europe has been discussed at the highest level.

Yours sincerely

Henry Wilberforce
Chief Executive
Harvard Plastics (UK)

funding Geldmittel
tax relief
  Steuererleichterung
skilled labour
  Fachpersonal
sound out
  aussondieren,
  herausfinden
AGM = Annual
  General Meeting
  Jahreshauptver-
  sammlung
confidential
  vertraulich

Ankündigung der Gründung einer Gesellschaft
Announcing the formation of a company

➡ Brief 99

Mediquip
Richmond Industrial Estate
Richmond
Surrey SU9 1JK
e-mail: mediquip@net.com.uk

12 July 20..

Krankenhaustechnik GmbH
Düsseldorfer Str. 90
45145 Essen
Germany

Dear Sirs

Medical and Surgical Instruments

We are pleased to announce that our newly formed company "Mediquip Ltd", Company Registration No. 2391824, will start trading in Europe as from September 1st.

We specialise in the manufacture and distribution of high-quality medical apparatus and surgical equipment. In addition, we pioneer innovative ideas by inviting selected customers to test new apparatus made available to them at a fraction of cost price, thus making new techniques and treatments available to patients at affordable prices.

Our latest invention is a device for kidney operations without major surgery. Besides this we are currently promoting a local anaesthetic package to cut down the risks associated with surgery normally performed under general anaesthetic.

We include our catalogue and export price list for your information. All prices are quoted FOB UK airport.

.../2

manufacture
Herstellung
distribution
Vertrieb
selected customers
ausgewählte Kunden
make available zur
Verfügung stellen
at a fraction of cost price zu einem
Bruchteil des Selbstkostenpreises
treatment
Behandlung
at affordable prices
zu Preisen, die man sich leisten kann
invention
Erfindung
device
Vorrichtung, Gerät
kidney operations
Nierenoperationen
promote fördern
anaesthetic package
Narkosepaket

143

Should you wish to be considered to take part in the testing of new devices please return the enclosed registration form. We would instal such devices at our own cost and offer attractive discounts on other orders to those participating.

We hope that we shall soon be able to supply you with your medical equipment needs. If you have any questions please do not hesitate to get in touch with us.

Yours faithfully
MEDIQUIP LTD

David Vance
Managing Director

Encs

cut down
  verringern
perform surgery
  chirurgische Eingriffe vornehmen
medical equipment needs
  Bedarf an medizinischer Ausrüstung

Gegenangebot
Counter-offer

➡ Brief 98

15 December 20..

Mediquip Ltd
Richmond Industrial Estate
RICHMOND
SU9 1JK
England

Dear Sirs

Your Offer No. 1093 for Surgical Instruments

Thank you for the above-mentioned offer of
December 1st.

We have studied your prices and compared them
with those of your competitors and, despite being
well pleased with the quality of the goods, must
point out that your prices are some 10% too high
for the market here.

If you can see your way clear to accommodating
us with a 10% reduction we will be pleased to
place an order for the equipment listed on the
order form enclosed.

We look forward to your response to our proposal.

Yours faithfully
DR. ZANDER KLINIKEN

Michael Schmidt
Manager

surgical instruments chirurgische Instrumente
compare vergleichen
competitor Konkurrent
be well pleased durchaus zufrieden sein
if you can see your way clear wenn Sie eine Möglichkeit sehen
accommodate s.o. j-m entgegenkommen
order form Auftragsformular
proposal Vorschlag

17 August 20..

Herrn Michael Bendorf
Am Neggenborn 80
44892 Bochum
Germany

Dear Herr Bendorf

Many thanks for your valued enquiry as regards our range of cabin cruisers.

I have mailed you our brochure today by separate post and I trust it will be of interest. The price list is effective from 1st September 20.. and is for UK specifications.

I have asked our importer, "Auto Theimann & Freizeit", Kohlenstr. 45, 44795 Bochum, Germany to confirm German prices, German specifications and also give you more detail about the products and built quality and other information you require.

In the meantime, if I can be of further assistance please contact me.

Yours sincerely
Mannepower International Ltd

Terence Perkins
Sales & Marketing Manager

c.c. Alfred Prentice

your valued enquiry Ihre geschätzte Anfrage
as regards hinsichtlich, betreffend
cabin cruiser Kabinenkreuzer
be effective gültig sein
specifications *hier:* Normen, Konstruktionsvorschriften
give more detail genauere Einzelheiten geben
built quality *hier:* Fertigungsqualität

Anhänge

Währungen verschiedener englischsprachiger Länder

Land	Währung		Abkür-zung	Unter-einheit
	deutsch	*englisch*		*englisch*
Australien	Austr. Dollar	Australian dollar	A$	100 cents
Bahamas	Bahama-Dollar	Bahamian dollar	B$	100 cents
Barbados	Barbados-Dollar	Barbados dollar	BD$	100 cents
Dominica	Ostkarib. Dollar	East Caribbean dollar	EC$	100 cents
Fidschi	Fidschi-Dollar	Fiji dollar	F$	100 cents
Großbritannien und Nordirland	Pfund Sterling	pound (sterling)	£ (stg)	100 pence
Guyana	Guyana-Dollar	Guyana dollar	G$	100 cents
Hongkong	Hongkong-Dollar	Hong Kong dollar	HK$	100 cents
Indien	Ind. Rupie	Indian rupee	Rs	100 paise
Irland	Euro	euro	€	100 cents
Jamaika	Jamaika-Dollar	Jamaican dollar	J$	100 cents
Kanada	Kanad. Dollar	Canadian dollar	C$	100 cents
Liberia	Liberianischer Dollar	Liberian dollar	L$	100 cents
Malawi	Malawi-Kwacha	Malawi kwacha	MK	100 tambala
Malaysia	Malaysischer Ringgit	ringgit	M$	100 sen
Malta	Maltesische Lira	lira, *pl.* liri	LM	100 cents
Mauritius	Mauritius-Rupie	Mauritius rupee	MauR	100 cents
Neuseeland	Neuseeland-Dollar	New Zealand dollar	NZ$	100 cents
Nigeria	Naira	naira	N	100 kobo
Sambia	Kwacha	Zambian kwacha	K	100 ngwee
Seychellen	Seychellen-Rupie	Seychelles rupee	SR	100 cents
Simbabwe	Simbabwe-Dollar	Zimbabwe dollar	Z$	100 cents
Singapur	Singapur-Dollar	Singapore dollar	S$	100 cents
Südafrika Republik	Rand	rand	R	100 cents
Tansania	Tansania-Shilling	Tanzanian shilling	Tsh	100 cents
Uganda	Uganda-Shilling	Uganda shilling	USh	100 cents
Vereinigte Staaten von Amerika	US-Dollar	United States dollar	(US) $	100 cents

Britische und amerikanische Maße und Gewichte

Längenmaße

1 inch	= 2,54 cm
1 foot	= 12 inches = 30,48 cm
1 yard	= 3 feet = 91,44 cm
1 (statute) mile	
	= 1760 yards = 1,609 km

Nautische Maße

1 fathom	= 6 feet = 1,829 m
1 nautical mile	
	= 1,852 km

Britische Hohlmaße

Trocken- und Flüssigkeitsmaße

1 gill	= 0,142 l	
1 pint	= 4 gills	= 0,568 l
1 quart	= 2 pints	= 1,136 l
1 gallon	= 4 quarts	= 4,5459 l
1 quarter	= 64 gallons	= 290,935 l

Trockenmaße

1 peck	= 2 gallons	= 9,092 l
1 bushel	= 4 pecks	= 36,368 l

Flüssigkeitsmaße

1 barrel	= 36 gallons	= 163,656 l

Amerikanische Hohlmaße

Trockenmaße

1 pint	= 0,5506 l	
1 quart	= 2 pints	= 1,1012 l
1 gallon	= 4 quarts	= 4,405 l
1 peck	= 2 gallons	= 8,8096 l
1 bushel	= 4 pecks	= 35,2383 l

Flüssigkeitsmaße

1 gill	= 0,1183 l	
1 pint	= 4 gills	= 0,4732 l
1 quart	= 2 pints	= 0,9464 l
1 gallon	= 4 quarts	= 3,7853 l
1 barrel	= 31.5 gallons	
	= 119,228 l	
1 barrel petroleum		
	= 42 gallons	= 158.97 l

Flächenmaße

1 square inch	= 6,452 cm^2
1 square foot	= 144 square inches
	= 929,029 cm^2
1 square yard	= 9 square feet
	= 8361,26 cm^2
1 acre	= 4840 square yards
	= 4046,8 m^2
1 square mile	= 640 acres
	= 259 ha = 2,59 km^2

Handelsgewichte

1 grain	= 0,0648 g	
1 dram	= 27.3438 grains	
	= 1,772 g	
1 ounce	= 16 drams	= 28,35 g
1 pound	= 16 ounces	= 453,59 g
1 hundredweight	= 1 quintal	
Brit.	= 112 pounds	
	= 50,802 kg	
Am.	= 100 pounds	
	= 45,359 kg	
1 long ton		
Brit.	= 20 hundredweight	
	= 1016,05 kg	
1 long ton		
Am.	= 20 hundredweight	
	= 907,185 kg	
1 stone	= 14 pounds	= 6,35 kg
1 quarter		
Brit.	= 28 pounds	
	= 12,701 kg	
Am.	= 25 pounds	
	= 11,339 kg	

Raummaße

1 cubic inch	= 16,387 cm^3
1 cubic foot	= 1728 cubic inches
	= 0,02832 m^3
1 cubic yard	= 27 cubic feet
	= 0,7646 m^3

Verzeichnis wichtiger Handelsabkürzungen

a.a.r.	against all risks	gegen alle Risiken
a/c	account	Konto
a/d	after date	nach Dato
AGM	annual general meeting	(Jahres-)Hauptversammlung
a.m.	ante meridiem	vormittags
approx.	approximately	ungefähr
art.	article	Artikel
A/S	account sales	Verkaufsabrechnung
ASAP	as soon as possible	möglichst bald
ATM	automated teller machine	Geldautomat
Bdy.	broadway	britische u. amerikanische Straßenbezeichnung
B/E (B(s)/E)	bill(s) of exchange	Wechsel, Tratte
B/L (B(s)/L)	bill(s) of lading	Konnossement, Seefrachtbrief
Bros.	brothers	Gebrüder
c./ca.	circa	ungefähr
CAD	cash against documents	Kasse gegen Dokumente
c.c.	carbon copy	Durchschrift
C.C.	charges collect	Erhebung von Gebühren, unfrei
CFR	cost and freight	Kosten und Fracht
CIF	cost insurance freight	Kosten Versicherung und Fracht
CIP	carriage and insurance paid to	frachtfrei versichert bis
c/o	care of	per Adresse
Co	company	Gesellschaft
COD	cash on delivery	Nachnahme
COS	cash on shipment	Zahlung bei Verschiffung
c.p.d.	charterer pays dues	Abgaben werden vom Charterer bezahlt
CPT	carriage paid to	frachtfrei
cr.	creditor	Gläubiger
c.r.	current rates	zu den Sätzen und Tarifen, die zurzeit in Kraft sind
Cres.	crescent	britische Straßenbezeichnung
c.t.	conference terms	Konferenzbedingungen
cv	curriculum vitae	Lebenslauf
cwt.	hundredweight	Zentner
D/A	deposit account	Sparkonto
D/A	documents against acceptance	Dokumente gegen Akzept
DAF	delivered at frontier	geliefert Grenze
d/d	days after date	Tage nach dato
DDP	delivered duty paid	geliefert verzollt
DDU	delivered duty unpaid	geliefert unverzollt

dep.	departure	Abreise, Abflugzeit
DEQ	delivered ex quay	geliefert ab Kai
DES	delivered ex ship	geliefert ab Schiff
div.	dividend	Dividende
doz.	dozen	Dutzend
D/P	documents against payment	Dokumente gegen Zahlung
Dr	Doctor	Doktor
d/s	days after sight	Tage nach Sicht
E.& O.E.	errors and omissions excepted	Irrtümer und Auslassungen vorbehalten
EEA	Exchange Equalisation Account	Devisen-/Währungsausgleichskonto
EFTPOS	Electronic funds transfer at the point of sale	Einzugsermächtigung am Kassenterminal
e.g.	exempli gratia, for example	zum Beispiel
EMS	European Monetary System	Europäisches Währungssystem
EMU	European Monetary Union	Europäische Währungsunion
encl, enc(s)	enclosure(s)	Anlage(n)
E.O.M.	end of month	Monatsende
ERM	Exchange Rate Mechanism	Wechselkursmechanismus
ETA	estimated time of arrival	planmäßige Ankunftszeit
etc.	et cetera, and so on	usw.
e.t.c.	expected to complete	zu erwartendes Löschende
e.t.s.	expect to sail	voraussichtliche Abfahrt
EXW	ex works	ab Werk
f.a.q.	fair average quality	Durchschnittsqualität
FAS	free alongside ship	frei Längsseite Seeschiff
FCA	free carrier	frei Frachtführer
FCR	forwarding agent's certificate of receipt	Spediteur-Übernahmebescheinigung
FCT	forwarding agent's certificate of transport	Spediteur-Übernahmebescheinigung
FIFO	first in first out	Zuerstentnahme der älteren Bestände
FOB	free on board	frei an Bord
FPA	free from particular average	frei von Teilschäden außer im Strandungsfall
ft. (')	foot, feet	Fuß
FTSE	Financial Times Stock Exchange Index	britischer Aktienindex
Gds.	gardens	britische Straßenbezeichnung
HGV	heavy goods vehicle	Lastkraftwagen (Lkw)
HMS	Her (His) Majesty's Ship (Steamer)	Ihrer (Seiner) Majestät Schiff (Dampfer)
H.P.	horse power	PS, Pferdestärke
HP	hire purchase	Mietkauf

ICC	institute cargo clauses	Versicherungsbedingungen für Gütertransporte
i.e.	id est, that is to say	das heißt
IMO	International Money Order	Internationale Zahlungsanweisung
in. (")	inch	Zoll
Inc.	incorporated with limited liability (AE)	GmbH, AG
incl.	including	einschließlich
INCOTERMS	International Commercial Terms	internationale Regeln für die Auslegung handelsüblicher Vertragsformeln
IOU	"I owe you"	Schuldschein
kg	kilogram	Kilogramm
lbs (lbs)	pound(s)	Pfund
L/C		
(L(S)/C)	letter(s) of credit	Akkreditiv
LIFO	last in first out	Zuerstentnahme der neuesten Bestände
Ltd	limited	mit beschränkter Haftung
m/d	months after date	Monate nach dato
MLR	minimum lending rate	Mindestdiskontsatz
M.O.	money order	Postanweisung
Mr	Mister	Herr
M/R	mate's receipt	Empfangsquittung, Bescheinigung, dass sich die Ware an Bord befindet
Mrs		Anrede einer verheirateten Frau
m/s	months after sight	Monate nach Sicht
Ms		Anrede einer Frau, ohne anzugeben, ob sie verheiratet ist oder nicht.
MS	motor ship	Motorschiff
MV	motor vessel	Motorschiff
N/A	not applicable	nicht zutreffend
No/Nos	number(s)	Nr.
O/o	to the order of	an die Order von
oz (oz(s))	ounce(s)	Unze(n)
p.a.	per annum	jährlich
pc (pc(s))	piece(s)	Stück
pd	paid	bezahlt
PIN	personal identity number	persönliche Geheimzahl
plc	public limited company	Aktien-, Kapitalgesellschaft
p.m.	post meridiem	nachmittags
P.O. Box	Post Office Box	Postfach
P.O.	postal order	Postanweisung

p.o.d.	paid on delivery	bezahlt bei Anlieferung
pp.	per pro (curationem)	im Auftrag; in Vertretung; per prokura
ppd	pre-paid	im Voraus bezahlt
p.t.o.	please turn over	bitte wenden
Pty	proprietary company, a private limited company registered in South Africa or Australia	GmbH
q.v.	quod vide	diesbezüglich siehe
recd.	received	erhalten
regd.	registered	eingeschrieben
R.O.G.	receipt of goods	Erhalt der Waren
R.P.	reply paid	Antwort bezahlt
rsvp	répondez s'il vous plaît	um Antwort wird gebeten
S/A	Statement of Account	Kontoauszug
sgd.	signed	gez., gezeichnet
Sqr.	square	Platz
SR&CC	(free from) strikes, riots and civil commotion	(Ausgeschlossen) Streik, Aufruhr und Bürgerunruhen
Through B/L, Thru B/L	through bill of lading	Durchkonnossement
T.T.	telegraphic transfer	telegraphische Überweisung
v.	vide	siehe
VAT	value added tax	Mehrwertsteuer
W(P)A	with (particular) average	Teilschaden ist mitversichert
WB, w/b	waybill (AE)	waybill
wt.	weight	Gewicht
yd.	yard	yard

Verzeichnis wichtiger Organisationen

BSI	British Standards Institution	Britischer Normenausschuss
BT	British Telecom	Britische Fernmeldegesellschaft
CBI	Confederation of British Industry	Britischer Arbeitgeberverband
EC	European Community	Europäische Gemeinschaft
ECB	European Central Bank	Europäische Zentralbank
EEA	European Economic Area	Europäischer Wirtschaftsraum
EEC	European Economic Community	Europäische Wirtschaftsgemein-schaft
EFTA	European Free Trade Association	Europäische Freihandelsgemein-schaft
EIB	European Investment Bank	Europäische Investitionsbank
ERP	European Recovery Programme	Europäisches Wiederaufbau-programm
ETUC	European Trade Union Confederation	Europäischer Gewerkschaftsbund
EU	European Union	Europäische Union
GATT	General Agreement on Tariffs and Trade	Allgemeines Zoll- und Handels-abkommen
GPO	General Post Office	Britische Post
IATA	International Air Transport Association	Internationaler Luftverkehrs-verband
IBCC	International Bureau of Chambers of Commerce	Internationales Büro der Handels-kammern
IBRD	International Bank for Re-construction and Development	Internationale Bank für Wieder-aufbau und Entwicklung
ICAO	International Civil Aviation Organisation	Internationale Zivilluftfahrts-organisation
ICC	International Chamber of Commerce	Internationale Handelskammer
IEA	International Energy Agency	Internationale Energieagentur
IMF	International Monetary Fund	Internationaler Währungsfonds

ISO	International Standards Organisation	Internationale Standardorganisation
MOT (test)	Ministry of Transport (Test)	Kraftfahrzeugüberwachungsamt (TÜV-Abnahme)
NAFTA	North American Free Trade Agreement	Nordamerikanisches Freihandelsabkommen
NATO	North Atlantic Treaty Organisation	Organisation des Nordatlantikpaktes
NCM-UK	NCM Credit Insurance Limited	Nachfolgerin der Versicherungsgruppe ECGD (Export Credit Guarantee Department) der brit. Regierung. Entspricht der deutschen Ausfuhrkreditversicherungsanstalt HERMES
OECD	Organisation for Economic Co-operation and Development	Organisation für wirtschaftliche Zusammenarbeit und Entwicklung
OPEC	Organisation of Petroleum Exporting Countries	Organisation Erdöl exportierender Länder
SITPRO	Simplification of International Trade Procedures Board	Behörde für die Vereinfachung internationaler Handelsverfahren
SWIFT	Society for Worldwide Interbank Financial Telecommunication	Gesellschaft für den internationalen Zahlungsverkehr zwischen Banken mittels Datenfernübertragung
TUC	Trades Union Congress	Britischer Gewerkschaftsbund
UNCED	United Nations Conference on Environment and Development	Umwelt- und Entwicklungskonferenz der Vereinten Nationen
UNCTAD	United Nations Conference on Trade and Development	Welthandels- und Entwicklungskonferenz der Vereinten Nationen
UNIDO	United Nations Industrial Development Organisation	Organisation der Vereinten Nationen für industrielle Entwicklung

Muster

1. Brief

LANCASHIRE ENTERPRISES plc

Enterprise House
17 Ribblesdale Place · Winckley Square
Preston PR1 3NA
Tel: (01772) 203020 · Fax (01772) 204129
Telex: 67257 LANENT G

Your ref.:   JB/lf
Our ref.:   Pa. 143.421

14 March 2005

Mr Johannes Becker
Europlastik GmbH
Postweg 7
D-82178 Puchheim
Germany

Dear Mr Becker

Your enquiry of 2 March 2005

Thank you very much for your recent enquiry about our products and those
of the firms we represent. We enclose our current catalogue and price lists,
together with our terms of delivery. Discounts are, of course, dependent on the
size of the order submitted.

We would be only too happy to send you samples of specific products, subject
to certain conditions, or to arrange for a representative to visit you and help
you to define your needs more closely. If you have any questions, please do not
hesitate to contact me or our Sales Manager, Annette Mason, at the telephone
number above. We look forward to hearing from you shortly.

Yours sincerely
Lancashire Enterprises plc

J. L. Palmerstone

J. L. Palmerstone
Managing Director

Enc

cc: Annette Mason, Sales Dept.

Lancashire House	Registered office:	Lancaster House
Watery Lane	Enterprise House · 17 Ribblesdale Place	36 rue Breydel
Preston PR2 2XE	Winckley Square · Preston PR1 3NA	1040 Brussels
Tel.: (01772) 203020	Registered in England and Wales No: 2401383	Belgium
Fax (01772) 721029	**A member of IMRO**	Tel: 32 2 230 34 38

2. Fax

CYBER INFORMATION SERVICE

Facsimile Cover Sheet

To:	Mirek Zlotkowski
Company:	Quantum Plus
From:	Lynn Dougherty
Phone:	+1 203-358-4389
Fax:	+1 203-358-4300
E-mail:	lynn.dougherty@cybernet.com
Date:	9/28/20..
Pages:	1 of 2

Comments:

I hope you enjoyed the National Center for Database Marketing Chicago Show as much as I did. I thought it was a great success because everyone was so enthusiastic and willing to share their experience, so we could all learn from one another.

I'm writing now with a special invitation to continue benefiting from the experience of your colleagues in database marketing. My marketing department has authorized me to extend to you a one-year subscription to the CYBER DATABASE for 20% off the normal subscription rate.

To order simply fax the attached Order Form or call our Order Hotline at 203-358-4355. We hope to hear from you soon.

Regards,

Lynn Dougherty
Lynn Dougherty
Senior Editor
Cyber Information Service

3. E-Mail

From:	PrecisionEngineering@webside.de
To:	merkur.gmbh@germanet.de
Date:	15 Oct 20..
Subject:	High Pressure Valves

Dear Mr. Merkur

Thank you very much for the samples of your high pressure valves, which we received on 15 April.

We were impressed by the quality of the valves but feel that they are rather expensive in comparison with similar equipment on offer from foreign competitors.

If you are able to reduce your prices by 10% we will place an order for 20,000 valves now and a further 10,000 in six months' time.

We look forward to your reply with interest.

Yours sincerely

Harold Thomas
Precision Engineering Co

4. Briefumschlag mit Anschrift in Großbritannien

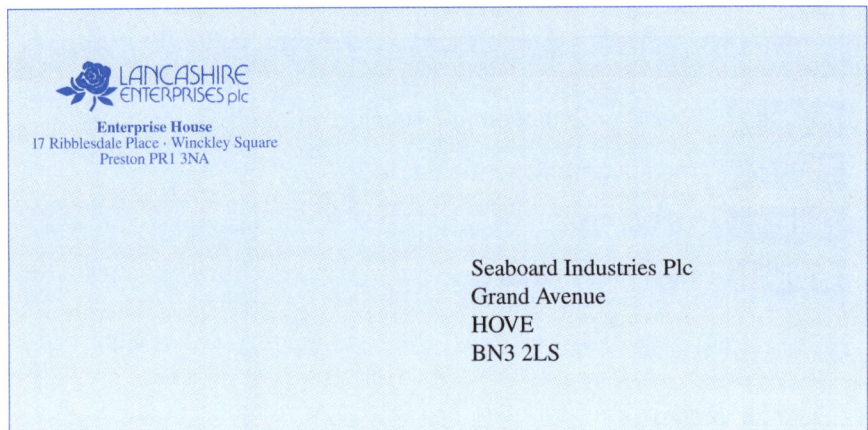

LANCASHIRE
ENTERPRISES plc

Enterprise House
17 Ribblesdale Place · Winckley Square
Preston PR1 3NA

Seaboard Industries Plc
Grand Avenue
HOVE
BN3 2LS

5. Briefumschlag mit Anschrift in den Vereinigten Staaten

The InterStay Hotel

1114 Seventh Avenue
New York, NY 10033

MR JOHN D ENRIGHT
COMPUTRONIC INC
PO BOX 8732
AUSTIN, TX 75110

Alphabetisches Sachregister

Die Tilde ~ steht für das halbfette Stichwort. Die Ziffern geben die Nummer des Briefes an.